own your space

own your space

ALEXANDRA GATER

**ATTAINABLE ROOM-BY-ROOM
DECORATING TIPS FOR
RENTERS AND HOMEOWNERS**

HARPER
DESIGN
An Imprint of HarperCollins Publishers

Photography by Lauren Kolyn

First published in 2023 by
Harper Design
An Imprint of HarperCollins *Publishers*
195 Broadway
New York, NY 10007
Tel: (212) 207-7000
Fax: (855) 746-6023
harperdesign@harpercollins.com
hc.com

Distributed throughout the world by
HarperCollins *Publishers*
195 Broadway, New York, NY 10007

ISBN 978-0-06-322820-7

Library of Congress Control Number: 2022944227

Cover and book design by Shubhani Sarkar
sarkardesignstudio.com

FOR GATER STUDIOS:
PRODUCER AND PROP STYLIST: Rayna Marlee Schwartz
MANAGER: Amanda Moroney
CONTRACTOR: Graham Hayes
MAKEOVER ASSISTANT: Alana Andrade
HAIR AND MAKEUP: Alanna Chelmick
ILLUSTRATION ON PAGE 37: spoak.com
ILLUSTRATIONS ON PAGES 53, 93, 120, 124: LeeAndra Cianci

Printed in Canada

First Printing 2023

Contents

PART
1 Planning

Introduction

I'M GOING TO LET YOU IN ON A SECRET: I'M NOT AN

interior designer. But hear me out. How many times have you flipped through a magazine or coffee-table book and found the most beautiful kitchen remodel and thought to yourself *One day, I will have a gorgeous kitchen just like that* even though the photo you are looking at is completely unattainable? Countless times, right? Here's the thing: I, just like you, love good design. In fact, I live, sleep, eat, and breathe looking at beautiful spaces created with budgets in the multi-thousands of dollars. Those projects fuel me creatively, and sometimes I, too, dream of the day when I can build and decorate a home completely from the ground up. But I'm also not someone who says *one day* when it comes to having a home that feels special. Our homes, whether rented or owned, are the places we live, sleep, laugh, dream, and work, and they're too important to say *one day*. I'm someone who says *today*, *this weekend*, *right now* is the time to make your dream home come to life, regardless of your experience with design.

Maybe you've just bought your first home and have no budget left to spend to remodel but really can't stand to look at those red oak kitchen cabinets for another day. Or maybe you're living in a tiny rental apartment and have no idea how to make it your own. Or maybe you've lived in the same place for a long time and are ready for a decor overhaul but don't know where to start. You've pored over hundreds of Pinterest images and dog-eared your favorite home tours in magazines but are still left with the question you set out to answer: How do I re-create this in my own space? This book will help answer that question.

Here's another secret: A few years ago, I hadn't painted a wall, picked out a rug, or styled a shelf. Now, I am a full-time entrepreneur who connects with millions of people on YouTube and Instagram on how to decorate their homes. You might be wondering how I got here, and although there were hundreds of little steps that landed me where I am today, in my mind it all started the morning I got laid off three years into my dream magazine job, just weeks after I went viral on YouTube.

After I graduated from university with a journalism degree and a minor in studio arts, my dream was to combine my love for photography and writing by telling stories through photojournalism. That's why I applied to intern in the graphic design department at *Chatelaine*, one of Canada's most celebrated women's lifestyle magazines, a brand that has been around for more than ninety years. About one week into the internship, I realized that laying out magazine spreads wasn't what I was meant to be doing (read: I was terrible at it). I bounced around between the art and editorial departments for a while, until one editor asked me to write content for the home section of the magazine's website.

I had absolutely no idea what I was doing, but quickly realized I loved it. I loved how a small, simple change like bringing a new duvet into my bedroom made my whole space feel brand new. I loved searching for fun products and fell in love with finding brands whose decor made me *feel* something. I was learning how to write service-driven magazine content and filing the tips and tricks I was picking up along the way in the back of my mind. It also made complete sense why I loved it so much: In all of the spaces that were mine up until that point (my bedroom in my family home with the twin bed pushed into the corner, my tiny dorm room in university, the hostel rooms I slept in as I backpacked my way through Europe), I was constantly seeking ways to inject comfort into them, because that was, and still is, what home represents to me—little woven lanterns wrapped around a curtain rod, a tiny throw rug to conceal gray-blue dorm room carpet, a sense of order in the backpack that held all of my belongings. Even though I was writing about things I really didn't know anything technical about, there was a familiarity there in every piece I wrote or online product roundup I curated.

Soon I was working on contract, assisting the home director of the magazine, and found myself on photo shoots, realizing I was living out the dream I had wanted for so long. I hadn't realized the dream I wanted looked like this, but it made so much sense: Turning a space into a beautiful image and seeing it in the glossy pages of a magazine was exactly the same feeling as composing a photo on my 35mm camera and having it developed. It was taking a mundane corner of an entryway and turning it into something truly beautiful with simple styling and getting the light to fall on it just so.

I'll gloss over the part in this story about how when I was hired full-time it wasn't to keep doing the job that I loved in the home department. Instead, I was assisting the editor in chief with daily admin tasks like organizing her calendar and booking boardrooms for staff meetings. Canadian magazine publishing was starting to fall apart, jobs were being cut, and there were about half of the people on the team compared to when I started. I kept assisting the home director while also working the admin role I was hired to do. I threw myself into home decor projects knowing that I'd have to find the time to get them done after hours. I knew I was young and lacked experience, but I also knew that if I didn't stick with the full-time position they offered me, there wouldn't be room for me on the team.

After about six months straddling these two roles, the home director left, and I was offered to take over the home section. I was shocked and excited and quickly realized I had to fake it until I made it. I was twenty-five and in charge of the entire home decor section of the magazine, producing photo shoots as well as writing and planning content for both online and print. It was a dream position and a new era for the magazine: The editor in chief wanted a fresh take on decor—budget-friendly, attainable solutions for those who didn't have thousands to spend on a room remodel like the other decor magazines boasted.

As one of the youngest editors on the team, I saw an opportunity to tap into the world of YouTube, where this younger audience that we wanted to appeal to was consuming buzzy, do-it-yourself (DIY) content that took a more laid-back and personal approach to home decor. These videos were all about the messy in-between process of a project and *not* being an expert. With that in mind, I began to see a gap in the world of home decor, and I pitched a video series all about helping millennials decorate on a budget. Other lifestyle magazines were reporting on celebrity home renovations, but where was the decorating advice for those of us who rented or didn't have a Hollywood-sized budget to drop on a remodel? As part of a generation who will likely be renting for longer than any other before us, I saw an opportunity.

That's when *The Home Primp* was born, an idea I had after watching countless hours of YouTube. I had been toying with the idea of starting my own channel for about a year,

but I couldn't land on what my niche was until I realized that I could expand the magazine content I was producing into video format. Alongside a team of videographers, I produced nineteen YouTube episodes over the span of a year for the magazine. I made over small rental apartments, bedrooms, and bathrooms, sticking to a tight budget and layering in lots of attainable decorating tips. Each video got on average two hundred to four hundred views on YouTube, until we published the second-to-last episode we would ever film. Over the span of about three weeks, this studio apartment makeover went from two hundred to six hundred to one thousand to just over *one million* views. I was on top of the world. I finally felt like I had found my place at the magazine, and I loved creating this video content and hosting the series. Everything was clicking into place. This was my dream job.

I have yet another secret: It sucks just as much as you think it would to get laid off from your dream job weeks after going viral on the internet. It sucks even more when you suffer from an anxiety disorder and your brain has trained you to think that bad things always strike when things feel just a little bit too good.

The studio makeover was still climbing in views, surpassing the one million mark, when I woke up to a calendar invite from the head of publishing in my inbox before eight in the morning. The subject "MANDATORY BUSINESS MEETING" was in all caps, and flagged with a red exclamation point as if to say "Read me right now!" I had planned to be running around the city that day prepping for a *Home Primp* shoot, not sitting in a conference room. There was no part of me that thought I was getting let go. I even jetted across the city in the opposite direction from my work to pick up a small rug for our shoot the next day.

When I arrived at the office, pink rug rolled up and tucked under my arm, the usual office buzz was replaced with hushed whispers, and everyone was huddled into small groups. The rumor was there was about to be a massive layoff. I had to be safe, right? My video had just gone viral, taking along every other episode of *The Home Primp* with it, as viewers binged the series.

But that didn't seem to matter. I got let go that day by a slew of executives in expensive suits who lined the glass conference room walls. The magazine was being sold to another publisher, and along with ninety other employees, I lost my job in the span of minutes. It was devastating and shocking. Having a video go viral is exhilarating, but for me it was more than that: I was doing something I loved and realizing that people *wanted* to see more.

In my mind, there was no way I could continue my YouTube career. Everything used to create these videos—the videographers, the expensive camera gear, the connections to brands that would send products, the channel itself—belonged to the magazine I was just let go from. That's why I felt a deep sense of devastation: None of it belonged to me, even though an hour before it was at the precipice of launching me into a world that really fulfilled me. But what I knew was that there was momentum created just weeks before, and that video was still going viral. The best thing I did without really even realizing it at the time was holding on to that momentum and starting my own channel.

A videographer friend of mine (the one whose space I had made over that went viral) had also lost her job, and she said she'd film and edit a few videos for me as a thank-you for the makeover. I made some connections in the YouTube world and signed with an influencer network in the hopes I could land some brand deals, and during that time I used my severance money to stay afloat. I did some freelance writing for a few home magazines and cohosted a YouTube series called *Buy or DIY* and poured that (tiny) amount of money I was making back into my channel.

Six months in, I had twenty thousand subscribers but still wasn't landing many paid campaigns, and my severance money had run out. Making YouTube videos in your bedroom is one thing, but producing makeovers is a whole other undertaking. It takes *a lot* of budget and camera and sound equipment—and a ton of time. I had dreams of growing my channel to a point where I could make it my full-time job, but in order to do that I knew I needed a team, which is what I had at the magazine. It felt really unattainable to start from scratch and do it on my own. For the first time in the six months after losing my job, I let myself think about applying for a full-time position and giving up my channel in its entirety.

About eight months into making YouTube videos on my own, I made a call to the influencer network I had signed with and told them I wanted to quit. I was embarrassed that I'd ever let anyone believe I could do this, including myself. I wasn't making money, I was lonely and unsure, and who starts a business without a business degree? (I have since learned that apparently tons of people do.)

Less than twenty-four hours after I made that phone call, I got an email that I had landed a brand deal that would fund my videos for the next six months. It's been a few years since I almost quit and then landed that deal. Since then, I have built a team of more than six full-time employees, an e-commerce business, and a channel that is watched by *millions* every month.

Just like life, design is messy and not linear. It's filled with trial and error, mistakes and disappointment, and hundreds of little steps that lead to a beautiful, finished room. It's always chaotic in the middle until suddenly all the cardboard is cleared off the floor and the dust is swept up to reveal a beautiful, shiny new space. When I think about getting let go that day, I can still feel the massive wave of unknown that was to come, kind of like when you roll the first coat of bold paint onto a wall and have no idea if it's going to look how you expected it would. But one of the best things I've ever done for myself was to keep going—even without the credentials or the experience—because it taught me not only how to create a beautiful space, but also how to sit in the unknown and create my dream career.

Here's the last secret I'm going to let you in on: Creating the home of your dreams might seem intimidating, messy, and daunting, but that's exactly the point. And you don't have to do this alone. This book is filled with step-by-step instructions for particularly tricky tasks, "psst" moments for quick bits of important info, and even "Snap and bring with you to shop!" buttons to give you something to refer to when finding the exact product you need at the hardware store seems a little too overwhelming. Are you ready? Let's get started.

PART

1 | Planning

A few months after I lost my job, I knew I had to move. I didn't have a steady income and had fallen into the world of entrepreneurship, but I got that feeling in the pit of my stomach that happens whenever I am faced with an opportunity that feels unexpected and at the same time imperative. They're the kind of chances that will fly by you if you don't latch on, the kind that could either be disastrous or life-altering, which is what makes them so scary. My friend texting me that she was moving out of her apartment of five years was one of those moments for me.

I knew and loved this apartment a lot. It was rented by friends before me, and years prior to me living there I would visit them and marvel at the brick wall and old ladder that reached the tiny storage loft. It was the kind of space I'm still drawn to now—one whose quirky charm creates effortless style, like the cool girl who makes sweatpants look chic. The apartment sits on the top floor of an old Victorian home in downtown Toronto. Light pours through every window, and the ceiling slants in odd places, following the shape of the roof. When you sit outside, an old tree strung with tiny patio lights leans over you, as if the deck was built around the trunk and you're sitting in the treetop.

The apartment, which I lovingly dubbed The Treehouse while I lived there, was my dream home. I have a visceral memory of standing on the back patio (which spanned the entire back of the house and was larger than my living room and kitchen combined) and looking into the living room. It was dark outside, but inside the table and floor lamps were on and lit the space with a warm, orange glow. It looked so cozy and so safe, and for the first time since I had moved in, it sunk in that this home was mine. While I lived there, I would sometimes think about how many times I had visited the apartment and not known that one day it would be mine, and what it would see. Over those two years, The Treehouse was shown off to television programs like *Cityline* and esteemed journalist Anna Maria Tremonti from the CBC, was a home for the last years of my seventeen-year-old cat Harriet's life and was where I experienced the end of a five-year relationship.

In many ways, The Treehouse also gifted me my career. I was able to completely make over the 500-square-foot space solely with reversible changes and document it for my new channel. It was my first time being a renter while also in the beginning stages of building a home decor business, so I had the time and freedom to experiment. As a renter, I learned what it meant to live in a tiny space with limited storage. I ran my business solely out of my home, which meant products for makeovers would be precariously stacked up the winding, narrow Victorian-esque staircase that led directly to my unit. I had to press my body against the railing to squeeze past baskets, vases, and sometimes live plants. In my actual apartment, I would hide practical things like luggage behind my bedroom

door and learned to live with clutter, like the time a brand I was working with accidentally sent me more than three hundred oranges for a shoot instead of one case. I also had the challenge of making the space my own within the confines of a strict lease agreement—one that stated I couldn't put even a tiny hole in the wall without permission—and spent a lot of time at the white dining table planning my next makeover, refresh, or big project.

I documented the transformation of making The Treehouse my own on my YouTube channel, naming the series *My Rental Reno*, and my subscriber count started climbing as viewers watched me install pink peel-and-stick backsplash tiles in my kitchen and convert the tiny living room closet into a home office (also known as the "cloffice"). That series was so successful that I ended up making over every room in my apartment twice.

Two seasons of *My Rental Reno* later, I went shopping at the grocery store right down the block from my apartment and saw the latest issue of *Chatelaine* at the checkout. Spanning the entire front page of the home section was a photo of my cat Lottie and me in The Treehouse, the subsequent pages outlining my tips and tricks for creating a home office in a small space. "Full-circle moment" can't fully capture what seeing that spread felt like, but that's what it was: tangible proof that getting let go from my dream job less than two years before was the best thing that could have ever happened to me.

Although so much of what you see in my YouTube videos is a polished transformation over two days, getting to the moment in my career where I was featured in the magazine I had been let go from was a process. And to this day, that's what most of my job is: prepping and doing lots of behind-the-scenes tasks like analyzing "before" photos, taking measurements, creating floor plans and moodboards, scouring product, picking paint colors, and spending way too much time on Instagram and Pinterest to ensure the best transformation possible.

The planning stage is the stuff they don't show you in magazines. It's a messy process, filled with trial and error, but one I find extremely rewarding and fun and that I hope you will, too. This section is undoubtedly the most important of the whole book because it goes through how to actually create a solid foundation for your makeover before you start putting paint on the walls or drilling holes. Whether you're moving into a new place (I'm sharing my secrets to finding a dream apartment if you haven't already), or want to refresh an existing room, this section will get you started by breaking down the behind-the-scenes process that all designers follow to create the dreamy spaces you marvel over every day.

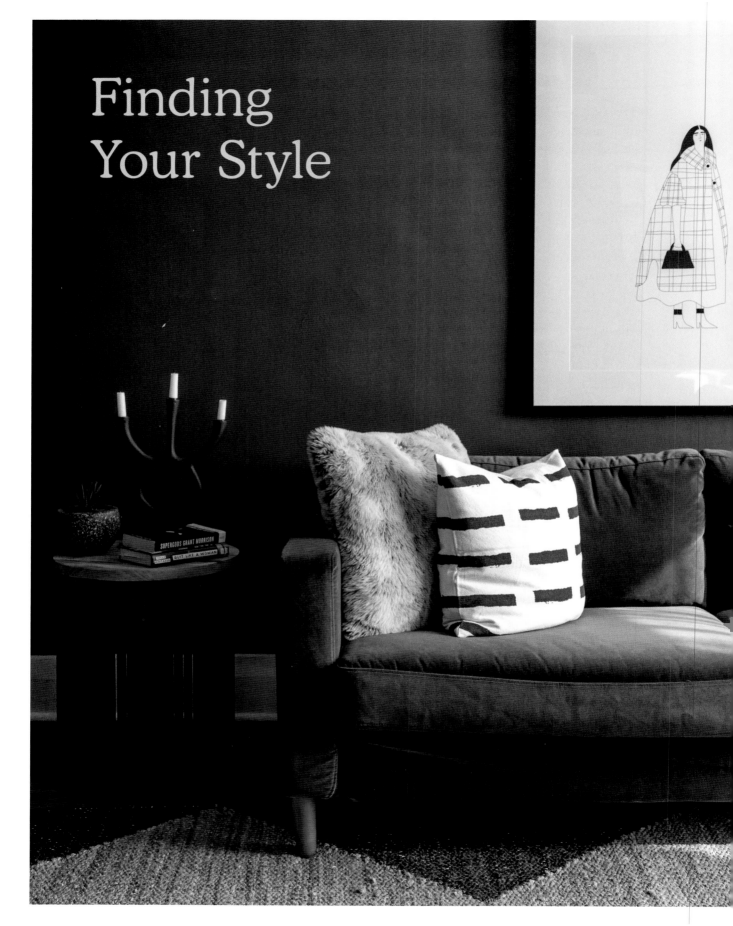

Finding
Your Style

GROWING UP, I ALWAYS ASSUMED THAT MY CLOTHING,

music, and design style all had to fit into one category, and I could never figure out which one I fell into. I knew what I liked, but it usually bridged many different styles, and I couldn't seem to stick to the confines of just one. As a teenager, that was confusing in a world where labels were everything, and I would have jumped at the opportunity to take a quiz that told me exactly who I should be and what group I fit into.

What's funny, though, is that it was years before I took a design quiz, even when I thought I had no idea what I was doing in my magazine home decor job. I was always sure of what I liked, and I never felt scared to trust that innate taste. I began to realize that a lot of the spaces I have a visceral reaction to are ones that have many design layers and don't fit into the neat box of just one style. With that said, putting names to the styles you gravitate toward the most can be so helpful when prepping your space. It can point you in the direction of retailers and design accounts that complement your style.

When people ask me what my style is, I usually throw out words like "eclectic" or "boho," but truthfully, some days I dream of living in a soft Scandi-style minimal home with all-white decor, and the next I'm sure I'm a maximalist. That's what I love about design, though: It's ever-changing and a constant experiment. When I moved into my first apartment, I didn't hold back from using the colors and patterns that I wanted to, regardless of what styles they fit into, and over the two years living there I made it over constantly. Allowing myself to experiment meant that I was purchasing what I loved, and design, for me, truly became a creative expression, rather than a mold I had to work within the confines of.

That's not to say that if you love rustic, farmhouse design you shouldn't fully embrace that—in fact if you know that's what you love, that *should* be the style you surround yourself with. But if you love farmhouse design and also a dash of boho, that's completely fine, too. Approaching design this way has also allowed me to have a dynamic space that I can build upon and continuously change.

So what is *your* style? This quiz will help you figure that out! I created this quiz to provide a ranking system, so rather than determining one style you're drawn to, the outcome of this quiz will rank your style preferences of popular design styles in order from most loved to least. Remember that this is just a starting point! There are tons more design styles out there to explore, but knowing what styles you are drawn to over others will give you a great idea of where to start.

Design QUIZ

RULES: All questions are yes/no statements. When you answer yes to a question, refer to the accompanying chart and allot a point to the design style indicated. If you answer no, do not record a point; move on to the next question. The styles with the most points are the ones you are most drawn to, and the fewest points the least. If you have a few styles that rank similar in score, it means you love a combination of them all and can finally create your own name for your inherently unique design genre.

1. You love color. Actually, love is an understatement. You can't get enough of it.

2. You prefer soft, floral, and striped patterns over loud, geometric shapes.

3. A pink-velvet sofa is the way to your heart (mine, too).

4. You love plants and would put them in just about every corner of your home if you could.

5. Style is secondary to you: A space that functions well is most important.

6. You like the idea of a fairly minimalist space, but won't compromise on elements of texture to keep it from feeling too cold.

7. Light floors over dark—always.

8. You love the way old and new pieces mix together. A modern white sofa paired with a reclaimed wood side table? *Chef's kiss*

9. White is a color? You don't know her.

10. You'll forage in your backyard for an interesting branch or piece of greenery before spending money on flowers.

11. Architectural elements like crown molding, exposed reclaimed wood beams, and wainscotting make you swoon.

12. When shopping for pieces to fill your space, you look for things to add function. Trends aren't usually for you!

13. Comfort can take a back seat when gorgeous Lucite furniture is involved.

14. You love style and you love comfort and won't compromise for one over the other: They can both exist at the same time.

15. You think the most unique spaces are ones that don't have a defined design style, but instead are a mix of eras and different design elements.

16. Teak furniture is your love language.

17. When you're at the paint store, you're comparing shades of white, cream, and gray—no color here!

18. Your design heroes are powerhouse women with styles similar to Shea McGee and Joanna Gaines.

19. You're really into arches, squiggles, and curved furniture—it's a vibe.

20. When looking at furniture, you prefer flat, clean lines (no bells and whistles here, please!).

21. Sometimes you think that you should have been born in the Gatsby era so you could throw exuberant parties in your lavishly decorated home.

22. What are rules? Clashing colors and patterns excites you.

23. Your dream space is an old loft with tons of exposed brick.

24. The thought of a space entirely decked out in white—white paint on the walls, white furniture, white walls—sounds like the most peaceful space ever to you.

25. Given two choices, you'd pick a throw adorned with fun shapes like squiggles and brightly colored shapes over something plain in a heartbeat.

POINTS SYSTEM

If you answered yes to these questions, allot a point to the following design styles:

Question 1:
Eclectic, maximalist, and boho design styles

Question 2:
Modern farmhouse and traditional design styles

Question 3:
Art deco and post-modern design styles

Question 4:
Eclectic, maximalist, and boho design styles

Question 5:
Industrial and minimalist design styles

Question 6:
Organic modern, mid-century modern, and Scandinavian design styles

Question 7:
Organic modern, mid-century modern, and Scandinavian design styles

Question 8:
Modern farmhouse and traditional design styles

Question 9:
Eclectic, maximalist, and boho design styles

Question 10:
Organic modern, mid-century modern, and Scandinavian design styles

Question 11:
Modern farmhouse and traditional design styles

Question 12:
Industrial and minimalist design styles

Question 13:
Art deco and post-modern design styles

Question 14:
Modern farmhouse and traditional design styles

Question 15:
Eclectic, maximalist, and boho design styles

Question 16:
Organic modern, mid-century modern, and Scandinavian design styles

Question 17:
Organic modern, mid-century modern, and Scandinavian design styles

Question 18:
Modern farmhouse and traditional design styles

Question 19:
Art deco and post-modern design styles

Question 20:
Industrial and minimalist design styles

Question 21:
Art deco and post-modern design styles

Question 22:
Eclectic, maximalist, and boho design styles

Question 23:
Industrial and minimalist design styles

Question 24:
Industrial and minimalist design styles

Question 25:
Art deco and post-modern design styles

RECORD YOUR POINTS HERE

Design Style	Points
Art deco and post-modern design styles	
Eclectic, maximalist, and boho design styles	
Industrial and minimalist design styles	
Modern farmhouse and traditional design styles	
Organic modern, mid-century modern, and Scandinavian design styles	

If You Are Drawn to
Art Deco and Post-Modern Design Styles

Bring on all the chunky furniture and plush, velvet fabrics. You're (boldly) stepping back in time with your love for both the Gatsby era and '70s design—maybe one more than the other, but it's fair to say you don't shy away from the bold, rich colors and intricately shaped furniture that can be found in **art deco** and **post-modern** design.

If you're drawn to plush, velvet fabrics and intricate, detailed patterns, you'll love the glamorous world of **art deco** design. Think mirrored surfaces, curved furniture, and statement lights. This style drips luxury and glamour.

If you love curved shapes, bright and bold colors (think intense, electric blues and yellows), and materials like Lucite, boucle, and brass, **post-modern** design is for you. Its playful shapes can be found in chunky furniture and fluted accents and '80s-inspired patterns like brightly colored shapes and squiggly lines. This style is fun and playful and prioritizes form over function. (Lucite chairs aren't the most comfortable to lounge on!)

If You Are Drawn to
Eclectic, Maximalist, and Boho Design Styles

If I could guess, you are someone who loves to break the rules when it comes to design and fashion. You love clashing patterns and color, and embrace texture and bold, loud hues. You love everything in excess, which is one of the key points of **eclectic, maximalist,** and **boho** design.

If you love elements from just about every interior design style, **eclectic** design might be for you, as it's the blend of many different styles to create a unique space. Though eclectic design often looks as though it's a mismatch of every design, color, and pattern, *good* eclectic design is carefully thought through. The best way to describe eclectic design is that nothing about it matches or "works," and yet somehow everything looks cohesive due to the intentional, unifying elements.

You might love the idea of putting a loud patterned wallpaper on the ceiling and a clashing-colored rug on the floor, à la **maximalist** design. With this style, more is more: more color, more pattern, and more texture. Like eclectic design, this style draws from a mismatch aesthetic but is less about blending styles and design eras and more about having fun with color and creating a bold, unique space.

If loud colors and patterns aren't your thing but you still love layering patterns and textures, you might be drawn to a softer approach to these styles with **boho** design, which is inspired by layering organic decor and natural elements with bold pops of color and pattern (and lots of plants!).

If You Are Drawn to
Industrial and Minimalist Design Styles

It's all about pragmatic, functional spaces for you. You're drawn to pared-down spaces with pieces that have flat, clean, sharp lines and minimal texture, often found in **industrial** and **minimalist** design.

If your dream space is a loft apartment with exposed brick and black steel windows, you're likely drawn to **industrial** design, in which spaces are filled with materials in iron, steel, stone, metal, and copper and matte black, gray, and white paint colors. You'll want to go for furniture in blocky shapes (like a large, square coffee table made from solid wood) and hooks or knobs made from old piping and pendant lights with exposed bulbs. Keeping things minimal, but functional, is key in this utilitarian style.

If you love the idea of a design style that is practical like industrial design, but gravitate instead toward brighter colors, **minimalist** design is for you. This is a style that uses white in almost every room to make the space feel open and airy. This style sticks with flat, clean lines to maximize space and make it feel open. This design style is often not about how a space looks, but instead how it feels and how the space is utilized.

If You Are Drawn to
Modern Farmhouse and Traditional Design Styles

You're a sucker for mixing old with new and revel in spaces that have architectural elements like ornate crown molding or wainscotting, which are commonly found in **traditional** design, or exposed reclaimed wooden beams, as in **modern farmhouse** spaces. You love vintage pieces and accessories that exude character, and value a space that feels comfortable and lived in.

If you are drawn to darker accent colors like black and decor pieces made from reclaimed wood (like barn-board benches) and wrought iron (think swooping multi-armed chandeliers with exposed candelabra bulbs), you'll love **modern farmhouse** design. Mixing modern furniture pieces with vintage accessories makes this design style feel less rustic than the traditional farmhouse style. It's comfy, laid-back, and casual but still current. Think: Joanna Gaines.

Like modern farmhouse design, **traditional** design is all about mixing comfort and style. Inspired by 18th and 19th-century European decor, spaces in this style will commonly use patterns like florals, stripes, and plaids and elegant accessories like gold lantern chandeliers. This style often uses dark woods and warm tones like reds and browns.

If You Are Drawn to
Organic Modern, Mid-Century Modern,
and Scandinavian Design Styles

One thing is true: You love bringing the outdoors in and are drawn to bright spaces that prioritize functionality. You're drawn to spaces with white- and cream-painted walls and furniture in natural, rustic woods, which can often be found in **organic modern, mid-century modern,** and **Scandinavian** design styles.

If you love minimalism, but don't shy away from layering lots of textures to make your space feel warm and comfortable, you'll love **organic modern** design, which features lots of cream and white, organic shapes, and curves in furniture (like round coffee tables) and natural elements like winding, delicate tree branches in a textured, plastered vase. Varying textures in throw blankets, rugs, and accessories is what makes these spaces feel comfortable and warm.

If you are drawn to spaces with elements like bare, painted white wood floors and an emphasis on natural light and materials, you'll love **Scandinavian** design (or Scandi, for short). Though you'll find textured elements in Scandi design, it is about creating a space that is uncluttered and minimal (think exposed lightbulbs and linen duvet covers). It's bright and airy, making it the perfect design style for layering in natural elements like greenery and rustic light-wood accents.

If bright and airy isn't your vibe but you still value simplicity and functionality, you're more likely to be drawn to **mid-century modern** design, which incorporates teak furniture, curved shapes, and clean lines. Though it's not as light and airy as Scandinavian or organic modern design and uses more pops of color, this design style still embraces natural elements and neutral colors on the wall.

Finding Your
Dream Rental Home

Snap and bring with you to shop!

MOST DAYS, I SCROLL THROUGH APARTMENT LISTINGS for fun. It's actually one of my most favorite pastimes because I love to envision how I'd transform them. When I look at a listing, I usually know right away if it's a winner because I've made over so many spaces. I now know just by looking at a space if it'll need a ton of money poured into it to make it look presentable. Depending on where you live in the world, finding a perfect, character-filled blank canvas that's also on budget is not always realistic (my friends and I joke that looking for an apartment can often be a full-time job). After looking at a series of kitchens with outdated cherrywood cabinets and laminate countertops that are the complete opposite of your style, you'll realize quickly that you're going to have to put some elbow grease into your new space to make it your own. So how do you sort through the thousands of listings online, or tell if the space you're eyeing has potential? I suggest breaking it down into two categories: things you can change with a little TLC, and things you can't. Your budget, preference, and DIY capabilities will determine if the space is right for you.

Things You Can Change with a Little TLC

Countertops: Check out the wear and tear on the kitchen and bathroom countertops. You can always put contact paper on old laminate countertops, but watch out for water damage or deteriorating surfaces. Making counters in such bad condition look nice isn't easy; sometimes they must be replaced entirely.

Kitchen cabinets: Take note of the cabinets' condition and finish. Are they paintable? If the cabinets are not solid wood—if they're laminate or engineered wood for example— they'll be harder to paint, but not impossible. You'll just need space to sand, prime, and paint them outdoors or in a garage. Look for signs of water damage and uneven surfaces—if the cabinets are in rough shape, they'll be harder to paint and will likely need to be replaced, which will put a dent in your budget.

Walls: Notice the paint color on the walls. Is the color of the walls too dark or the wrong color for you? Don't be disheartened; you can always paint them (and I will encourage you to do that throughout this book!). During your tour, remember to ask the owner if you can paint. Painting is one of the biggest game changers in a space, and if it's off the table, this could be a deal breaker.

Character: Try to overlook the current tenant's furniture and search for details that make a space special. It's usually a space's architectural windows, brick walls, ornate molding, and old wooden floors that make it stand out from other rentals. Listings with character are always the ones I pause at and take time to scroll through or take time to view in person.

Lighting: How do you feel about the lighting? Lighting is one of the easiest things to upgrade. For example, if the rental you're touring is filled with blue-hued overhead lighting, it might make the space feel colder than it actually is. Simply switching out the existing bulbs can make a space feel completely different (and instantly cozier!).

Tile: The tile in a kitchen or bathroom might be outdated in a cute, granny-chic kind of way, or it could completely miss the mark. Backsplash tile in a bathroom or kitchen is easy to hide with peel-and-stick products. You can put a temporary backsplash over just about any tile, unless it's very uneven and bumpy.

Storage: How many closets are there? No matter how much of a minimalist you think you are, and no matter how much purging you do before your move, you will always need more storage. There are plenty of clever ways to add storage in a rental, but if you are touring a home or apartment that doesn't have a single closet, consider if this situation will actually be realistic for you to live with.

Things That Are More Difficult to Change

Floors: Look down and take note! My first apartment was filled with dark, cherrywood floors. Although they were the exact opposite of my preferred style (it's light hardwood for me, all the way), the space got so much sunlight, and there were tons of other winning selling points like the skylight in the kitchen and the massive brick wall that I knew would distract from the floors. Ask yourself: *Are there ways I can decorate around the floors, like using a large rug to cover them? Will my overall decor style distract from the color?*

Kitchen cabinets: If your landlord won't let you paint the cabinets, ask yourself if living without your dream of a pink kitchen is okay with you. If the existing cabinets are a neutral color like white or gray, you can always add renter-friendly additions like a temporary backsplash or new cabinet hardware to add color and pattern.

Carpet: If the rental you are looking at is decked out with wall-to-wall carpet, consider this a permanent fixture you'll have to live with. Removing carpet is a costly and timely change to make because once it's removed, you have to deal with what's underneath it. (It's not always those dreamy hardwood floors you are hoping for!)

Appliances: Oftentimes you don't have to worry about the look of appliances in a kitchen because their standard colors (white, silver, black) allow you to design around them.

What to Do Right After You've Moved In

There are a few things you can do once you move into your new home that will drastically transform it even before you start decorating. Whenever I make over a space, we do three things before we start decorating—and it's these three simple things the clients always notice first when they open their eyes and see their new space for the first time. If you can get into your space before the move-in date, I'd recommend doing these things before your space is filled with furniture:

Patch holes: Go around your entire space and fill any holes in the walls left by previous tenants. (See page 56 to learn how to spackle a hole.)

Paint the walls white: I cannot stress this one enough. Even if your walls are already white (though I bet they're renter's beige) but haven't been painted since the last tenant, paint them white again (see page 64 for my favorite white paint colors). Painting your space a fresh, crisp white will make it feel brighter and cleaner.

Change out your lights and lightbulbs: This can be done once you move in, and hiring an electrician for an hour doesn't cost a ton of money. You'll be amazed at what a difference getting rid of those rental fixtures makes! Make sure to store the old fixtures (and label what room they came from) so you can take the lights you've invested in with you when you move. Don't underestimate the power of simply changing out a bulb—a warm hue will make your home feel much more inviting.

Asking Permission from Your Landlord to Make Permanent Changes

In all the spaces that I've rented, whenever I've proposed a plan that is beyond renter-friendly changes (like the kitchen makeover in my current apartment on page 150), I've always found that landlords are excited about the prospect of having a tenant who will improve their property value, but they always ask these two questions: What is the plan, and who is making the changes? In both the rentals I've lived in, the landlords have been excited to contribute to the cost of materials and labor once they've understood my vision. You want to present them with a solid plan, a breakdown of costs for materials and labor, and a product list. The best-case scenario is that they'll see the benefit in upgrading their property and contribute to the cost. The worst-case scenario is that they'll say no. In most cases I've found that landlords want to do the labor themselves or have people they know do it, but if you have a contractor or handyperson whom you can suggest, make sure to include that name, too.

Here is a letter template that you can copy and paste by scanning the QR code at the bottom of the page. Use this as a starting point to get the conversation with your landlord going.

Dear (*insert name of your landlord*),

I am so excited about moving into this new home!

I'm writing to you with some proposed changes I'd love to implement in my (*name the room*).

To start, I'd love to (*list exactly what changes you'd like to make. Be as specific as possible. I suggest breaking it down into permanent changes and reversible ones, too*).

I plan to stay in this apartment for some time, and I have a passion for home decor, so I am confident I can make changes that will benefit us both.

I've come up with a plan that I have shared with you below, breaking down the products I've sourced and cost of materials, as well as a moodboard so you get an idea of how everything will look in the space. If you agree with these changes, please let me know if you approve of me doing the labor myself or if you have someone you would prefer. I would love to chat with you about splitting the cost of materials, if I am going to cover the labor.

I am confident these changes will greatly improve the (*insert room*), and I look forward to hearing your thoughts!

(*Your name*)

Does your rental have dark floors? Use a light rug to brighten the space.

Where to Find a Handyperson to Make Changes

I'm not going to sugarcoat it: One of the biggest struggles I had for years when it came to executing makeovers on my channel was finding a reliable and skilled handyperson to assist on makeover day. *Where did you find that handyperson?* is still a common question I get asked almost daily. Once you find someone you trust, the opportunity to really make your space your own won't seem so daunting.

Here's where to start:

Ask your landlord if there's anyone they trust and prefer you work with.

Ask friends for recommendations. Word of mouth is how most of these relationships come to be.

Try an online or mobile service like TaskRabbit, where you can find a handyperson based on the project, like building furniture or handling electrical wiring.

Check your neighborhood or condo group forum to find and contact people who have had work done to their units.

Floor Plans

When you think of floor plans, you might picture technical drawings and blueprints. Leave those to the experts. Like a moodboard, a floor plan is a must when making over a space—but don't worry, yours can be a lot simpler than an architect's. When I started making over people's homes, I didn't make floor plans, which in the early days of my channel meant *a lot* of re-ordering and last-minute problem-solving once I actually got into the space.

Digital floor plans have allowed me to get more creative with my designs because they help me make my ideas visually come to life before I start ordering products. A to-scale, digital mock-up of your room allows you to experiment with furniture placement and catch any gaps in the design. Seeing a loveseat in a floor plan, for example, might help you realize that you *do* have space for a shelving unit for extra storage, versus the full-size sofa that would take up the entire wall.

Before I even start on the design, I make a quick sketch on my iPad or in a notebook of the space I am making over and write in the measurements of each wall. I mark where the windows, electrical outlets, and doors are. Once I have my sketch, I re-create it with a digital floor plan tool. There are so many of these programs online for beginners, and most are really intuitive, easy to use, and free. Many of these programs allow you to drag 3D icons of furniture and accessories into the plan, and you can input their actual measurements to see how they will fill the space. I find this particularly helpful when I can't figure out what size rug to buy, or how my sofa will look floating in the middle of the room as opposed to against the wall.

Remember to measure the furniture you are using in your new space when you take down initial measurements!

Floor Plan Programs for Beginners

Spoak
SmartDraw
RoomSketcher

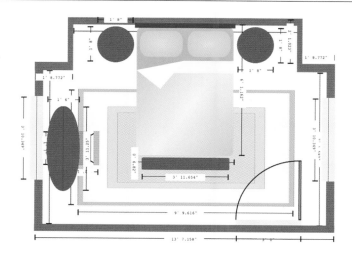

Moodboards

Whenever you are planning a makeover of any size, you'll want a moodboard. People often feel stuck with figuring out what to purchase based on the colors of items they already have, but it will feel much less overwhelming if you can visualize all of the elements like furniture, accessories, and paint colors together.

Often people think of moodboards as a collection of inspirational images, and although that's a great way of nailing a certain style, I pull in actual products that I am thinking of adding to my space. I find it helpful to see how all my products look beside one another. It's amazing how many times I've thought something will look good and then once I moodboard it, I realize the colors or styles don't work together. Swap different options in and out until you land on a combination that feels good. Once you've found the combination you love, make sure your pieces will fit by adding them into your digital floor plan. The best part is, this moodboard will become your shopping list!

Moodboards are also a great way to keep ideas organized—there's such an overwhelming amount of content online and in magazines that it can be difficult to keep up. My rule of thumb is that I am selective about what I save on my phone, on Instagram, or on Pinterest—but I *always* save an image if it makes me feel something. That might sound awfully poetic, but that's the best way for me to describe it. If a space makes me feel excited or inspired, or if I think *That is my dream space*, I'll save it. If it doesn't make me feel at least two of those things, I don't. Fun fact: I have a folder on my desktop called "My Dream Home" with about ten images in it. This is the folder reserved *only* for images and ideas that I don't want to forget or lose. If you see an image in a magazine, try and find it online (most print articles can be found online!) or take a photo of it with your phone.

Moodboard Programs I Love

SOFTWARE YOU CAN DOWNLOAD	WEBSITES YOU CAN ACCESS
Microsoft PowerPoint	Milanote
Microsoft Word	Canva
Adobe Photoshop	Spoak

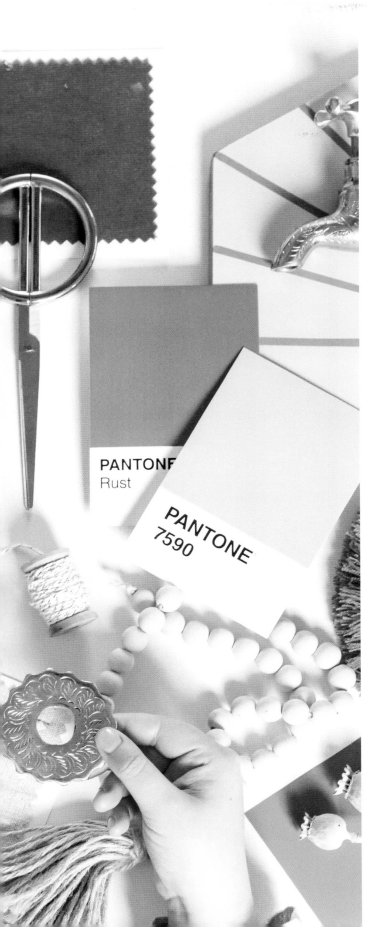

Things to Add to Your Moodboard

Paint colors

Existing items you are reusing in the space. This is an important step for seeing how both old and new pieces will work together! Try looking up product images online, or upload photos of them from your phone.

All new products you are purchasing (rugs, lighting, art, furniture, accessories).

Inspiration images. Try to narrow these down to three images of spaces that you really, really love. I find too *much* inspiration can clutter up the vision you're actually going for.

A "before" image of your space, so you can refer to it as you're moodboarding.

Don't know where to start? Find one inspiration image that you love and one piece of decor that you are dying to own (like a rug, sofa, art—anything!) and build from there. Or pick a color and weave that into a few of the pieces you choose—a few consistent colors will keep your space looking cohesive.

Planning a Shared Space

Psst *When you're picking paint colors with your partner or roommate, browse online for interiors painted in the color you love and have them do the same. Seeing a picture of what the paint on the wall looks like, rather than in a digital swatch, will help you both visualize better.*

MOVING IN WITH A

partner or roommates is already challenging. Add decorating decisions into the mix, and things can get complicated, especially if you are living with people who don't like the same things as you. How do you make a home look cohesive when you're living with someone who has completely different tastes than you? Here are my tips on designing a space that feels consistent but caters to more than one style. If you are feeling stuck and frustrated, know that decorating with someone else who has opposite tastes than you do is a challenge that many of my viewers face.

Start by communicating about your make-or-breaks: Is there a specific color that is off limits? Are there pieces that must be included in the design? Take note of these.

When my partner and I moved in together in the apartment where I live now, we were so hung up on our respective, opposite decor styles that we didn't know how our home was ever going to represent us both.

Instead of ruminating on our favorite design styles, Noah and I found it really helpful to instead pick pieces we were drawn to, outside of any labels. Instead of getting boxed into specific design styles, focus on pieces you love. Start with a list of retailers you both agree on, and start browsing. Drag all of your top selects into your moodboard. Do the same thing with paint colors, rugs, and accessories.

Once you've both thrown your picks into the moodboard, you'll be left with an assortment of colors, patterns, and styles, which means it's time to edit. Start by removing pieces you don't both love, until you land with an assortment of pieces that you do. You should start to see a board that is a meld of both of your styles.

If you find that everything is just seeming like a cluttered mismatch, hone in on one or two colors you can agree on and weave that color throughout the board in your products to create consistency.

Remember that this is an evolving process, and it might take you awhile to agree on an assortment of pieces you both love.

But what if your partner or roommate is drawn to a *completely* different style than you are, and you can't seem to land on any compromise? I hear you. When I moved in with Noah, I had just come from an airy, pink, and bright space while his had had dark navy blue walls and lots of industrial touches. It was really difficult for both of us to imagine how our styles were going to come together, especially because the color palettes we loved were on opposite sides of the spectrum.

As we started combining our styles and pushing each other out of our respective comfort zones, we began to realize that it's absolutely possible to mix a light and dark palette and still land somewhere in the middle. Since moving in together, I've been incorporating more darker tones into our home, and I love how it has added depth to my style and helped it evolve.

> **Psst** *If you're designing a space with someone who is not as passionate about home decor as you are and therefore has trouble visualizing, showing them photos of rooms that represent your dream space will help them imagine how the changes will look.*

Color Combos That Work Well Together for a Variety of Styles

I used to be someone who thought that there was no way to mix light and dark colors and end up with an airy, soft design. But as my design style evolved—and after I moved in with someone who does not, in fact, love pink as much as I do—I began to expand my color palette and realized that oftentimes mixing dark and light colors actually leads to a really eclectic mix of styles. I hope these give you some inspo so that you feel like you can have pinks *and also* blacks in your home.

If you love pink tones but your partner loves dark tones, mix pinks with terra-cottas, browns, and pops of black and gray. The terra-cottas and browns ground the pinks and make them feel less delicate.

COLORS:
Dusty rose and light pink, cognac brown, muted gray, warm terra-cotta, jet black

Navy blue and pink is such a winning combination and looks beautiful paired with soft gray accents. Don't overlook the effect patterns have on your dominant color scheme: The vintage rug pattern in a blue-gray makes the blue and pink combo feel more worldly and mature.

COLORS:
Muted pink, navy blue, soft cream, rusty red, blue-gray

This is a great example of how you can have a bright and colorful piece of furniture in your space without it being the focal point. Layering in complementary hues of taupe and mustard makes the pink less of a dominant color and more of a supporting act (in the best way).

COLORS:
Blush pink, mustard yellow, navy blue, smoky taupe, leaf green

If you've decided on a mostly dark space, layering in different hues of charcoal and off-blacks will make the design feel more dynamic. Peachy pinks and cream will soften it while adding in a tiny hit of color without compromising on the refined style you're likely going for.

COLORS:
Off-black, charcoal, sandy cream, peachy pink, bright navy

Toolkit

What You'll Need

I know tools can be intimidating, but before you skip over this section, I'm here to tell you that you only need to buy a few basic tools and hardware before you start decorating. I've tried to narrow the list down to the things you'll need to do the basics—like hang art, spackle a hole, and hang a shelf. Knowing what you will need to add to your kit will come with each project you tackle, but this is a good starting point.

A. Drill and a few drill bits (see page 55 for drill bit sizes I recommend)

B. Some basic anchors and screws (see page 55 for anchors and screw sizes I recommend)

C. Screwdriver that comes with a few basic bits

D. Hammer

E. Level (large and small)

F. Tape measure

G. Ruler

H. Scissors

I. Utility knife

THINGS TO ADD TO YOUR KIT IF YOU SEE YOURSELF DOING MORE-INVOLVED DIYS:

Wrench

Pliers

Wire cutters

Staple gun

Voltage pen

Stud finder

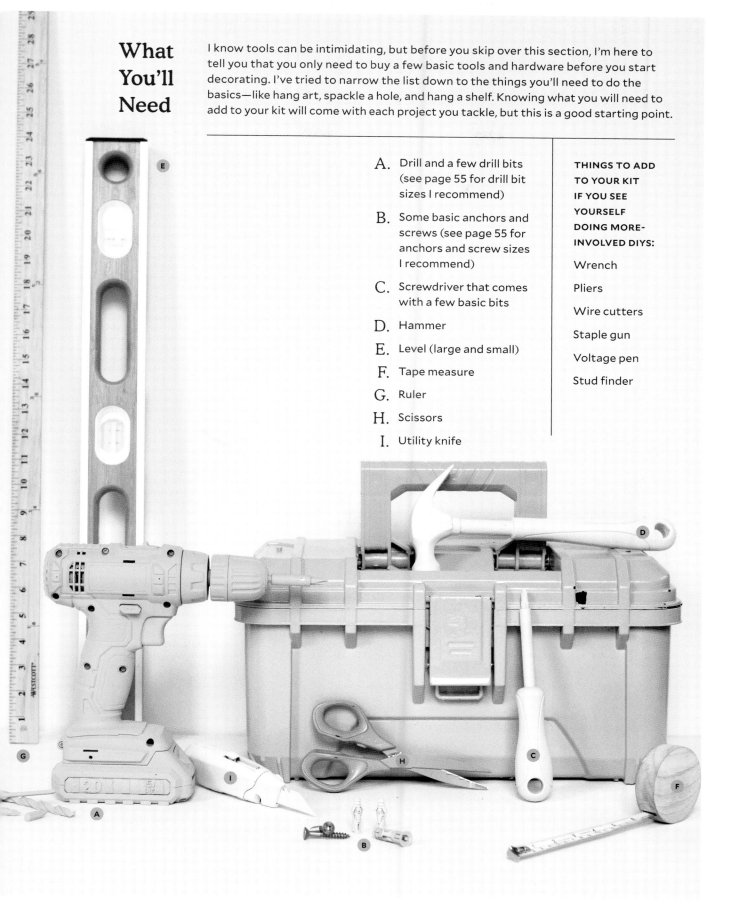

Paint Kit

You'll also want a mini paint kit, which should contain the following: (See pages 88–89 to learn how to paint.)

(See pages 88–89 to learn how to paint.)

Snap and bring with you to shop!

A. Drop cloth

B. Rollers: one small and one regular size, with roller cages

C. Paint tray with liners: one for brush, one for roller

D. Painter's tape

E. Brushes: one angled brush and one flat (size depends on the wall, but 3 inches [7.62 centimeters] wide will work for most)

F. Rag

G. Spackle knife, spackle, and sandpaper or sanding block

H. Foam brush

I. Paint pole

HOW TO | Read a Tape Measure

Knowing how to read a tape measure means that you can properly plan and ensure that the furniture you are ordering fits in the space you are decorating, and that means you will have to measure accurately. Whenever you measure something, make sure that the silver end of the tape is wrapped around the edge of a wall, or flush against it if that's not possible. This illustration will help you read your tape measure and ensure you're writing down the exact measurement each time.

> **Psst** *Make sure your tape measure is straight and level whenever you're measuring something to ensure accuracy!*

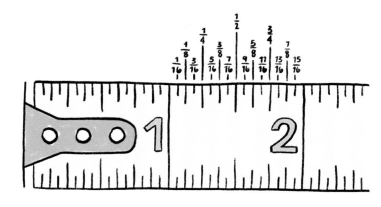

HOW TO | Use a Level

Before you hang anything, you want to make sure it's sitting straight on your wall using a tool called a spirit level. You want to place the level on top of the horizontal item you're leveling (like a shelf or frame) and make sure the bubble is sitting evenly between the two guidelines. Tilt your object to the left or right to get the bubble to move.

If you're drawing a straight line on a wall, place your level on the wall either vertically or horizontally until the bubble is sitting evenly between the two guidelines. Hold the level firmly in place and use a pencil to draw a line across the top of the level and on to the wall.

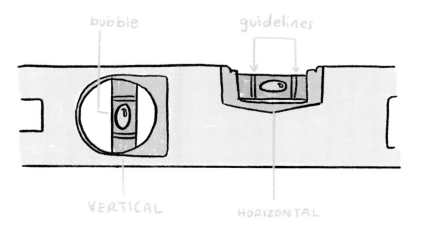

HOW TO | Use Wall Anchors

Whenever you are hanging something on the wall, you're going to want to secure it—an anchor is the way to go if you can't locate a stud in your wall (honestly, locating a stud is difficult without the right tools, so always just assume you'll need an anchor). Fun fact: Screws aren't meant for drywall or tile, so they won't stay in the wall securely without the help of an anchor.

1

2

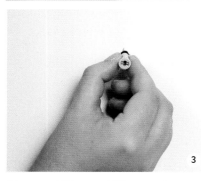

3

4

WHAT YOU'LL NEED

Anchors

Screws

Two drill bits (one that matches the size of the anchor you'll be using

and one that matches the size of the screw head you'll be using)

Drill

Hammer

INSTRUCTIONS

1. First, pick what kind of anchor you're going to use. (See page 55 for the suggested kind of anchor you should use depending on your project.)

2. Drill a hole using the drill bit that matches the anchor thickness you've picked.

3. Place your anchor in the hole.

4. Lightly tap the anchor in with a hammer until it's flush to the wall.

5. Using the drill, change the bit to one that matches the screw head and lightly drill the screw into the anchor.

Psst Choose the anchor based on your wall's material, and then pick the weight that you need, which is dependent on what you are hanging.

Anchors 101

A. **Drywall anchors:** These are the most common, come with many decor items, and are usually yellow. Use these to hang lightweight things such as picture frames. They are ideal for drywall, plaster, cement, and wood.

B. **Expansion anchors:** These will hold much more than a generic drywall anchor and are good for hanging medium-weight things like wall hooks and towel bars. They are ideal for drywall, plaster, cement, and wood.

C. **Self-drilling anchors:** Use these if you don't have all the tools needed for installation, such as a drill or drill bits. You just need a screwdriver to put these in the wall. They will usually hold up to 75 pounds (34 kg). They are ideal for drywall, and espeically in ceilings.

All About Drill Bits

Now that you've picked your anchor, you're going to need a drill bit (unless of course you're using the self-drilling kind). The kind of drill bit you need depends on what material you're drilling into, and the drill bit's size depends on the anchor weight rating you need to use for the project. When you're buying your anchors, look for the drill bit size written on the package.

A. **Masonry and tile drill bits:** Used for brick, stone, concrete, and ceramic tile. Avoid using a regular drill when drilling into brick, stone, or concrete. Instead use a a drill with a hammer function, or rent one, from the hardware store for one-off projects.

B. **Twist drill bit:** Used for wood, drywall, some metal, and plaster. This is the drill bit you'll use for most common household projects.

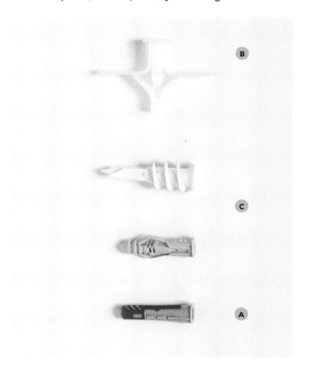

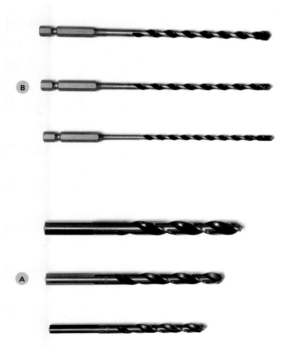

Snap and bring with you to shop!

HOW TO | Spackle a Hole

One of the easiest ways to revert your rental back to its original state is by patching holes you create in the walls. All you need is some sandpaper, a spackle knife, and some pre-mixed spackle. Spackling a hole just requires a few easy steps.

You'll likely notice at the hardware store that there's both white spackle and pink spackle, and the color will be indicated on the packaging. I like using the pink one because when the spackle dries, it turns white, letting me know when it's dry.

1

2

3

4

WHAT YOU'LL NEED

Sandpaper or sanding block

Lint-free cloth

Spackle

Spackle knife

Paint in the existing wall color

Small paintbrush

INSTRUCTIONS

1. Sand down the hole with fine-grit sandpaper or a sanding block. Wipe it down with the lint-free cloth to get rid of any dust.

2. Put a small amount of spackle on your spackle knife and spread it over the hole in your wall. Let it dry completely.

3. Once completely dry, sand the spackle until it's smooth. Wipe any dust away with the lint-free cloth.

4. Paint over the patch with the existing wall color.

> ***Psst*** *Optional: Depending on what you plan to keep on the shelf, you might opt for using brackets to offer more support. You can purchase these at the hardware store, or your shelf might come with them.*

HOW TO

Hang a Shelf

Shelves can be used for just about anything—decorating or storage or both!—and are a super functional way to fill a blank wall. Now that you've got some anchors and drill bits in your toolkit, it's time to learn how to hang a shelf. Once you've mastered this, you'll likely feel confident to hang just about anything.

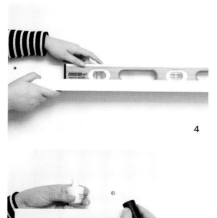

WHAT YOU'LL NEED

Long level

Pencil

Drill

Drill bit

Anchor

Screws

Hammer

Nail polish that matches shelf color

INSTRUCTIONS

1. Draw a straight, horizontal line using a long level with a pencil at the place where you want the shelf to sit. (See page 53 on how to use a level.)

2. Hold your shelf up along the line and, with a pencil, make marks aligned to the screw holes in the shelf. If you're using brackets, have someone help you hold the brackets up underneath the shelf, place a level on top of the shelf, and once it is straight, make marks in the bracket holes.

3. Drill the holes with a drill bit, and hammer in an anchor. Screw in one side of the shelf.

4. Once one side is screwed into the wall, hold the shelf with one hand and use a level to make sure the shelf is level. Then screw the other side into the wall.

5. Use nail polish that matches the shelf to hide the screws!

HOW TO | Hang Art Using Painter's Tape

Hanging anything that needs two screws can be challenging to get right with one try. This hack makes it super simple.

WHAT YOU'LL NEED

Pencil

Tape measure

Long level

Painter's tape

Marker

Screws or nails, depending on how heavy your art is

INSTRUCTIONS

1. Find the spot on the wall where you want the top of the art to sit and use a pencil to make a mark.

2. Place a piece of painter's tape across the back of the frame from edge to edge and mark dots where the hangers are.

3. Measure the distance from the top of the frame to the picture hangers and measure that same distance on the wall under the mark you made in step 1.

4. Using a level, draw a straight, leveled line across the mark you made in step 3.

5. Remove the painter's tape from the back of the art and stick it to the wall, aligned along the line. Drill screws or hammer nails where the dots are. Remove the painter's tape.

6. Hang your art!

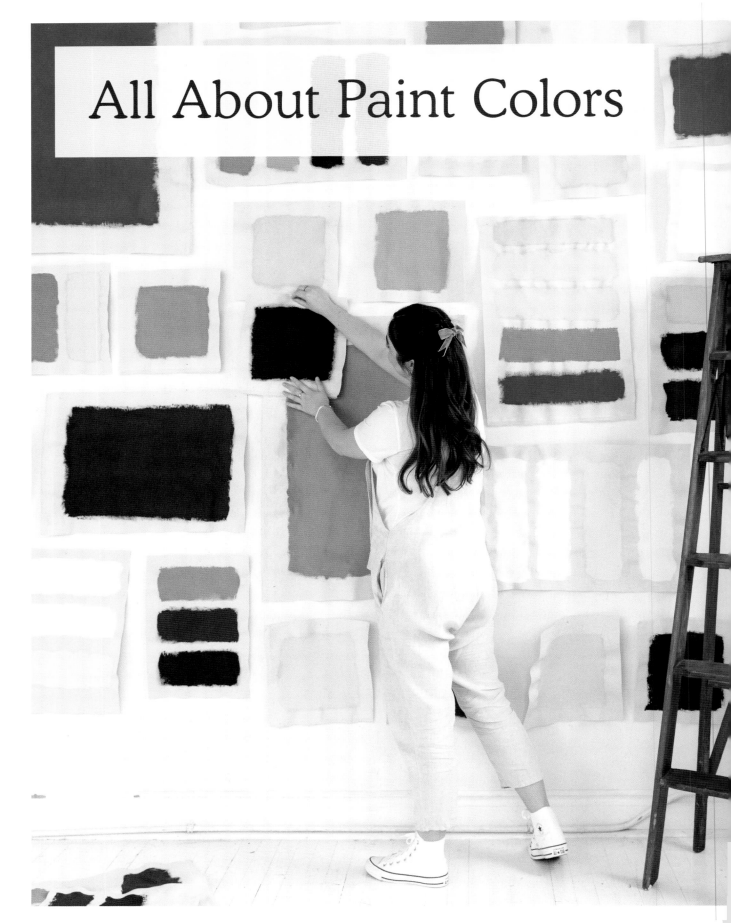

All About Paint Colors

I USED TO BE SO INTIMIDATED BY PAINT. THERE WAS A
point where I flat-out avoided it because there are *thousands* of paint colors to choose from:
How was I supposed to know if the white I picked wasn't going to skew too yellow? Where
did I even start looking for colors I liked? As I started to do more makeovers on my YouTube
channel, I noticed that the most impactful before-and-afters, and the videos that were the most
well-received by viewers, were ones that incorporated bold paint colors. It makes sense: Paint is
hands down the *easiest* and most budget-friendly way to transform a space. And you don't even
have to use color on your walls to make an impact. Just painting your walls white will instantly
make your home feel bright and fresh. Paint no longer overwhelms me, but that's because
I've experimented a lot. I've swatched countless color samples, I've painted the same room a
million different pinks (true story, though a million is an exaggeration), and I've slowly built
a group of colors that are my go-tos, which I'm excited to share with you in this section.

Picking the Right Shade

Here are my basic tips when picking a paint color for your home (so you don't have to paint
your room multiple times to get it right).

If you're a paint newbie and have no idea where to start, create a moodboard filled with
images of rooms painted in colors you love. Call this your personal paint palette, if you
will. I love going to smaller paint brands with a curated selection of colors, like Clare and
Backdrop, so I don't feel overwhelmed.

Once you've found a color you want to paint your room (let's say blue, for example), start
poring over inspiration online until you find a shade in a space that you fall in love with.
If you can find the name and brand of it, grab a sample and paint a swatch on your wall.

There's nothing better than finding a room painted the color of your dreams, with the paint
hue listed by the designer. When that's not the case, hunting down the color is difficult but not
impossible. I once found the dreamiest photo of a pink door—the pink was perfectly dusty, not
too pastel, had undertones of gray, and was sophisticated instead of juvenile—but I couldn't
for the life of me find the color name. I printed the photo of the door and brought it to my local
hardware store. Most paint specialists will be able to color match it closely. If you know the paint
name and color code, the hardware store should be able to mix it, regardless of what brand it's
from. If there's a wall in your home that's already painted and you love the color but don't know
what it is, bring a small chip of it (use a utility knife to get the chip from an inconspicuous
spot on the wall, like behind an electrical outlet) for the hardware store to match; they'll use a
special machine that essentially scans the color and matches it exactly.

Keep a record of colors that you love by noting the color name and code in one place, like
in a photo album on your phone. You don't have to keep old paint cans to do this. Instead,
take a photo of the top of the paint can where it says the color and code and save it to a folder
named for the room it'll be used in.

Test your color by painting a swatch on the wall and live with it for a few days. Pay
attention to how the light throughout the day affects the color.

Psst *If you don't want to paint a swatch on your wall, you can buy peel-and-stick paint swatches! Some individual paint companies sell these for less than five dollars each. If they don't, there are smaller companies, like Samplize, that sell peel-and-stick samples with colors from a variety of paint companies to choose from.*

My Favorite Paint Colors

Picking *one* paint color can be difficult, but choosing multiple colors? That's basically a full-time job. Don't worry, I've taken the guesswork out for you by showing you some of my favorite hues. My paint library is always expanding, but it's taken a while to curate a palette of colors that I turn to time and time again, which is why I wanted to share my tried-and-true favorites with you.

Snap and bring with you to shop!

My Favorite Whites

PURE WHITE, SHERWIN-WILLIAMS:

If you're looking for a plain white—a white white—this one's for you.

MASCARPONE, BENJAMIN MOORE:

If you're looking for something warm but not dark, this is it. It reads almost beige, without being too yellow. This is a great neutral that isn't a pure white!

SIMPLY WHITE, BENJAMIN MOORE:

Because of its yellow undertones, this is a warm, creamy white (note that it doesn't read "yellow"!) I use this in almost all of the rooms I make over.

STRAND OF PEARLS, BENJAMIN MOORE:

This buttery white skews a bit country/rustic and looks so good with gold hardware.

My Favorite Almost Blacks

GRAPHITE, BENJAMIN MOORE:

If you're looking for something dark and moody but still soft, this color is for you. It also looks amazing on the exterior of houses. See this color in action in Rayna's bedroom on page 170.

GRAY OWL, BENJAMIN MOORE:

A classic, neutral gray. This is a great neutral that isn't white!

White paint with yellow undertones skews warmer, while blue undertones will result in a cooler white. If you're not sure which temperature of white will work in your space, consider the other colors you are working with. If you have lots of warm colors, like reds and oranges in your space, a warmer white makes sense. Blues, greens, and purples work best with a cooler white. There are also "pure white" paint colors with no undertones other than white. These whites are crisp, stark, and work best with modern decor or on trim.

HALE NAVY, BENJAMIN MOORE:

The perfect navy, deep and rich.

My Favorite Pinks/Purples/Reds

KALAHARI SUNSET, BEHR:
A terra-cotta hue that's rich without being too red or orange.

SULKING ROOM PINK, FARROW & BALL:
Gray undertones make this mauve color look sophisticated and bold.

MODERN LOVE, BACKDROP:
This is MY pink! It's muted, dusty, and has some gray, which takes the juvenile feeling out of it.

SOUTHERN COMFORT, BENJAMIN MOORE:
Pinker than Modern Love, this is a rich pink that has undertones of brown, so it doesn't feel too pastel.

GOOD INTENTIONS, BACKDROP:
If you love purple but don't want your bedroom to read "eight-year-old," this is a great option. It's a gorgeous neutral lilac with gray undertones. This is a great neutral that isn't white!

My Favorite Greens

PIGEON, FARROW & BALL:

In darker light, this color reads gray with subtle green undertones. In brighter light (like in my kitchen), this is more of a true green.

COOL CURRENT, SICO:

This is the perfect sage green and feels grown-up, while still fun. This is a great neutral that isn't white! Light greens often show up on a wall much paler than they appear on the paint chip, so if you're looking for something a little more pigmented, go a shade or two darker.

SALAMANDER, BENJAMIN MOORE:

The best way to describe this color is that it looks like the depths of a lake. It's rich, deep, and a great cross between green and navy.

WINDSOR GREEN, BENJAMIN MOORE:

A hunter green alternative and the perfect deep, olive green.

My Favorite
Color Palettes

You've got your wall colors picked,
but now how do you ensure that the
furniture you're going to add to the
space matches? I've created some of my favorite
palettes of colors that look amazing
together. Take them with you when out
shopping, and stick within the hues here
so your design stays consistent.

Snap and bring with you to shop!

Neutral

CREAMS, WARM GRAYS, OFF-WHITES, SAGE GREENS, RUST REDS

Pair these colors with these materials:

Stone   Light oak wood

Bold & Colorful

DUSTY PINKS, PEACHES, GRAY-BLUES,
CREAMY WHITES, CHARCOALS

Pair these colors with these materials:

Olive-green velvet   Antique brass

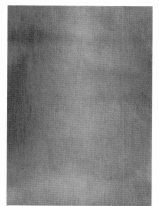

Dark & Moody

CHARCOALS, NAVY BLUES, EGGPLANT PURPLES, TAUPES, CREAMS

Pair these colors with these materials:

Dark walnut   Bronze

Bright, Airy, & Colorful

MUTED PINKS, WARM WHITES, LILACS, SAGE GREENS, CHARCOALS

Pair these colors with these materials:

Gold   Mustard velvet

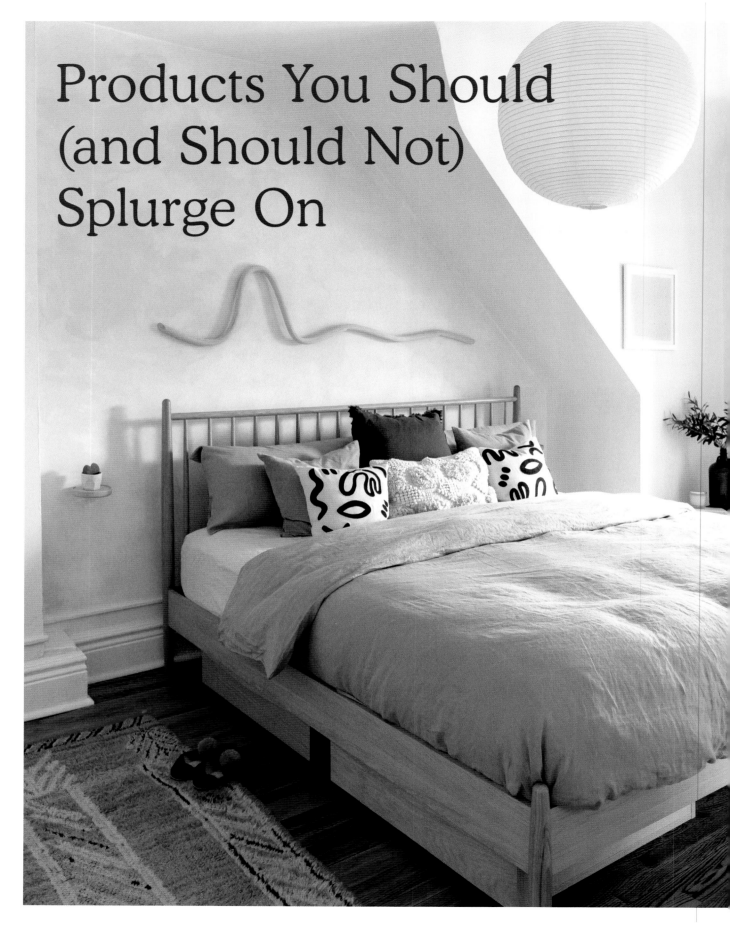

Products You Should (and Should Not) Splurge On

TRENDS IN DESIGN ARE, IN ONE WORD, FUN, AND IF

you're a decor enthusiast like me, you know that resisting trends can be difficult. Often in the videos I put out on my channel every week, there is a nod to at least one trend circling around the design world to keep the content entertaining and relevant. Something I've learned with my evolving sense of style is that good design doesn't rely solely on trends but instead on timeless pieces that allow you to layer in those more of-the-moment accessories whenever you feel like it. But what about those larger purchases? Should you drop a lot of money on that green-velvet sofa you really love, and if so, what if it becomes outdated in a few years? Furniture and decor add up quickly, and it's so easy to get caught up in trends, so I've curated a solid list of what items are worth splurging on and which aren't.

Splurge

Sofas: Splurge on either the sofa itself or a decorative cover. You can never go wrong with a neutral-colored sofa. It will adapt with you and your style and is easy to accessorize. Most sofas that are comfy and good quality will be a splurge, but this is a piece you want to last. But what if you *really* want that pink-velvet sofa? Head to page 198 to see my solution to investing in a piece that won't date in a few years—no matter what color it is.

Throw cushion inserts: The secret to any well-styled sofa is its accompanying throw cushions and, most important, their inserts. Inexpensive inserts will flatten quickly after a few uses, become uncomfortable, and won't show off your beautiful cushion covers. Look for something full that will hold shapes (if you karate-chop it at the top and it stays compressed, this is a good indication). Try and stay away from Poly-Fil—you can't sink into this kind of material, and it doesn't hold shape—and instead choose a microfiber down fill. Buy a larger insert for your cushion cover (at least 2 inches [5 cm] larger) to make your cushion look fuller.

Area rugs: In my opinion, a rug really makes or breaks a room, and I find that lower-quality fabrics can instantly downgrade the level of sophistication of your space. If it's made from a low-quality synthetic material or if there's a pattern printed on top of the rug, rather than woven into it, don't expect there to be a high durability. Rugs made from natural fibers like wool or jute are far more expensive but will last you a very long time and look amazing in your space, too. This rule also applies to outdoor rugs—splurge on a weather-resistant material like polypropylene and be able to enjoy it in your outdoor space year after year.

A good coffee table or dining table: When I moved into my first apartment, I bought a small dining table secondhand, but it never sat properly and wobbled whenever I sat down, no matter how many times I adjusted it. A solid, well-made table will last you years, and if you get something neutral (bonus points if it's wood!) it will stay timeless and match lots of different styles. If you don't live in a big space and are eating at your coffee table, the same rule stands. Plus, a coffee table is going to be in the center of your space, so you want it to really shine.

Decorative pendant lights: In just about every makeover I do, I talk about the power of lighting, especially in a small space. I love to add an oversized, large pendant light, especially when I'm transforming tiny apartments, because they are a statement and usually complete a space. Because pendants take center stage in a room, spend a little more on one that you really love.

Good bedding: Although I love a good patterned bedspread (I still remember a floral duvet cover I had in my childhood bedroom—I was obsessed), nothing beats a neutral set of linen sheets. Linen is expensive, but there are so many pros: It is more breathable than a lot of other fabrics, which means linen sheets keep you cool in the summer and warm in the winter; it is naturally hypoallergenic; and linen gets softer every time you wash it. A neutral color will allow you to add trendy pieces like throw cushions and blankets whenever you feel like a change.

Servingware: I've never regretted having a solid set of good-quality servingware, with plenty of bowls and trays. I've had my fair share of trendy salad bowls, but I always seem to reach for my good set of neutral, quality ones so it all looks uniform. Accessorizing with napkins, napkin rings, and fun tablecloths is a great way to partake in trends and a less expensive way to customize your table.

Cutlery: This might sound like a strange thing to splurge on, but I've learned this tip the hard way! When I moved into my first apartment, I bought gold cutlery with pink handles, and I loved it. It was inexpensive, and I bought about three sets so I could have dinner parties. These pieces quickly started chipping—first the pink handles and then the gold color—and they soon reflected the price I paid for them. What I learned is that good-quality cutlery is expensive, but will last years.

Pottery: I have a thing for ceramics, and I think it's because I've discovered so many amazing artisans who are creating really unique pieces. I love knowing where each item is made, and I've started a collection of handmade decorative items like ceramic knots and patterned, irregular-shaped mugs that I have on display around my home. These pieces won't go out of style because they double as art and are one of a kind.

Don't Splurge

Throw cushion covers: If you've got a great insert, your throw cushions are going to make your sofa pop regardless of how much you spend on the covers. I would encourage you to not invest in covers, as they are a piece that you can use to play with trends since they can be easily switched out. Cushion covers are a great way to achieve a specific style in your space without dropping thousands on new furniture.

Decorative accessories: Unless you're buying a coveted accessory from your favorite designer (see my note on pottery above!), don't splurge on the finishing touches. This can be anything from cushion covers and throw blankets to vases and candle holders. Think

of these items as the trendsetters that can be changed whenever you feel like it. These are the smaller styling accessories that are easier to switch up than a full-size sofa.

Table lamps: Get trendy with your table lamps. I treat most table lamps and floor lamps as an extension of every other decor accessory. There are so many fun ones on the market, and they're a great way to inject personality into a space. They're also an easy thing to switch up when you want to refresh.

Glassware: You can never go wrong with simple, inexpensive cups. They will break, and you will need to replace them. It's not worth splurging on the type of stuff you'd find in your grandmother's china cabinet!

Side tables or end tables: These don't have to be a focal point of your space. You really just need something simple to place a glass of water on, so they don't need to be a huge investment.

Runners: My reasons for suggesting to splurge on area rugs don't apply to runners. Chances are, small runner rugs will end up in high-traffic areas like your entryway or in your kitchen, so their lifespan will automatically be shorter. If you can snag an affordable runner that's made from cotton and is machine washable, that's all the better.

PART

2 | Decorating

Decorating people's apartments has become second nature in a lot of ways, simply because I've done it so often. My team and I are a well-oiled machine and can anticipate all the problems (which do still arise on every single shoot, if you're wondering!) and react with a quick solution. When I'm making over my own space, I can go at my own pace, but filming it for YouTube means we pack weeks of work into three long days.

We ask the makeover recipient to relocate for those few days so we can transform their home and then reveal the new space to them. Reveals are *always* nerve-wracking for both of us, and I don't think there's been a single makeover where I haven't felt butterflies when we stood together, their eyes closed and ready to see their new home. On three, their eyes open, and almost everyone says *I can't believe I live here.*

Out of all the makeovers I've done, the most memorable reaction actually didn't happen during the reveal, but instead when the camera stopped rolling. The makeover was a tiny studio apartment transformation, and the tenant had been nominated by his friend, so I was revealing it to them both. Before the reveal, when the camera was being set up, I made small talk with them in the hall. They told me they were going out for dinner after we wrapped. After the reveal, when the camera was turned off and my team and I started packing up, I heard the homeowner say to his friend, *Let's eat here instead, I don't want to leave this space* as they popped champagne to mark this new clean slate. The moment of them clinking glasses is a memory that comes back to me often, because it sums up exactly why I do what I do. Before the makeover, he got rid of almost every piece of furniture he owned because he was ready for a fresh start, and for the first time in five years, his space finally felt like his. He didn't just love how it looked, but he also wanted to *be* in it. This was worth celebrating.

Home decor, to me, is so much more than making something look beautiful or owning the nicest sofa on the market. Decorating for me has always been, and continues to be, more of a feeling. It's feeling safe and good in your surroundings. It's feeling like your home is a direct reflection of *you*. It's feeling like you don't want to leave. And the best part, I've realized, is that sometimes it's the smallest things—like lighting a new candle or getting into a freshly made bed adorned with your favorite sheets—that bring this feeling to us.

For me, the makeover reveal happens when there's still cardboard on the floor and paint supplies in the corner, when either a plant is placed or a light is hung and I can't just see the vision coming together but I can *feel* it, too. And it's this feeling that I've come to realize is what makes these transformations so special.

This feeling is what makes these makeovers easy to execute over and over again. The truth is, I find my work more satisfying than anything I've done before because the process is so creative and always rewarding. Watching how one coat of white paint makes a room look instantly brighter and the ceilings taller, or how switching a layout suddenly breathes new life into a room, never gets old. I'm surprised every time we're done, not because I ever doubted it would look great, but because the end result is always the complete opposite of where we started.

I credit a lot of my success to the people who have trusted me enough in their homes during the early stages of building my channel. Those whose living rooms I placed rugs in that were too small, and left curtains too long they were pooling on the floor (and not in a cute way). It took me years and a lot of trial and error—which is now permanently archived for anyone on the internet to see at any time—to learn that making a space that elicits that *wow* reaction is in the million little decisions that you don't notice. It's in the precise length of curtains, the finish that's chosen for the wall paint, the hue of the lightbulb in the decorative table lamp on the side table. It's in the size of a rug and the height you hang an art piece.

It's these details that I think keep people from feeling like design is attainable, and that's the reason I refuse to call them "rules." But just like I did, you will find yourself at the paint counter being asked what sheen of paint you'd like, and standing in the aisle at the hardware store wondering how it's possible there are so many lightbulbs to choose from. My goal in this section is to collect all the tiny details I've learned *not* to miss in my makeovers and put them in one place so it makes the process a little easier for you to feel those goosebumps when you walk into your new space.

Decorating with Paint

Snap and bring with you to shop!

YOU'VE ALREADY GOT THE SUPPLIES NEEDED TO PAINT

a room (see page 52), and hopefully you've narrowed down your palette and picked out some great paint colors, so now it's time to lay down your drop cloth and start the first step in your decorating process.

Paint is arguably one of the most transformative ways to update a space, and luckily it's also one of the most cost-effective, too. I love using paint to add color to a space, but I also love using it functionally, especially when it comes to visually dividing an open space. Painting can seem intimidating, but once you do it a couple of times, it's easy to get the hang of it.

Sheens of Paint

When you walk into any paint or hardware store, you'll be asked what kind of paint you'd like and what sheen, and the answer depends on where you're using it. Use this guide for your next painting project.

Flat/matte: This is the "flattest" finish of paint, with no shine. It's a trendy, modern choice for walls but it isn't very durable. Matte paint is difficult to clean, so it's best to use it in low-traffic areas or on ceilings. I once painted the back of a bathroom door with matte paint and was in love with the look, but the novelty wore off about a week after. The door became scratched, rough to the touch, and stained with water marks because it was where we hung towels.
PROS: Covers wall imperfections, color is very pigmented, gives a sophisticated and modern look
CONS: Not very durable in high-traffic areas, scuffs easily
USE IT: In bedrooms (but not kids' rooms!), in dining rooms, or on ceilings

Eggshell: This is the finish I use most often when painting interior walls because it's low-shine, but more durable and easier to clean than a flat/matte finish.
PROS: Gives the look of a matte finish but is much more durable and a DIY favorite
CONS: Can be difficult to touch up in small areas seamlessly
USE IT: Just about anywhere

Semigloss/high gloss: These finishes are the shiniest of all the paint sheens and are usually not used on interior walls. When used on a wall, the finish looks very glossy (which is definitely a look if you're into that!). These finishes of paint are used mostly on baseboards and trim. If you're painting your kitchen cabinets, this is also the finish for you.
PROS: Easy to clean and perfect for high-traffic areas like baseboards and cabinet fronts
CONS: If you use glossy paint on a wall with lots of texture and imperfections, these marks will be enhanced
USE IT: To paint window and wall trim, bathrooms, baseboards, and kitchen cabinets

Kinds of Paint

Water-based: The most common kind of paint, also known as latex paint. Durable but not as durable as oil-based paint. Used most commonly in houses on walls or trim.

Oil-based: More for high-traffic areas like kitchens and doorways. Always use it to paint furniture (including Ikea pieces!) unless you're using limwash or chalky paint.

Chalky paint: Not to be confused with chalkboard paint! Chalky paint gets its name from the fact that it dries with a chalky, matte finish and is most commonly used to paint furniture. DIYers love it because you can use it on just about any surface. You can also use a bit of sand paper to scuff it up and create a rustic, vintage-looking finish.

Limewash paint: I love limewash. It's been around for years (even before latex paint existed!) and is made by burning crushed limestone, then mixing it with water to create a paste, and finally adding natural color. Free of the chemicals called volatile organic compounds (VOCs) found in regular paint, limewash is a natural way to add color and create a plastered, textured look.

Paint

My best tips to make painting your
wall the easiest (and prettiest) ever.

*Use an
extended
roller. This
will make
painting so
much quicker!*

WHAT YOU'LL NEED

Refer to the paint kit on page 52.

INSTRUCTIONS

1. Prep! It's tedious, but prepping your space before you paint should never be a step that's skipped or it will result in a messy-looking job. Remove electrical outlet covers and put down a drop cloth and dust the wall with a lint-free cloth. Use soap and water to clean the wall. Also remember to wear something that you don't mind getting permanently stained. No matter how big or small your project, you'll likely walk away with paint splatters on your clothing.

    Tip: If you skip this step, any dust that's present will mix with the paint and you'll be able to see the texture of it on the wall.

2. Use painter's tape to cover the areas you don't want to paint, like baseboards and trim.

3. Put a fresh liner in your paint tray and pour paint. I always start with a little bit of paint in my tray and add more as needed.

4. Dip your angled brush into the paint and pat the brush against the sides of the tray to get some of the excess paint off the brush.

5. Holding the angled brush like a pencil, paint a straight horizontal or vertical line where your painter's tape meets the wall. This is called "cutting in" and will provide a good outline to roll within.

    Tip: Buy good-quality painter's tape for a few dollars more. If you cheap out on it, it won't stick to your wall and the paint will bleed under it, resulting in a messy line.

6. Switching to a roller brush, roll the roller brush into the well of the paint tray to load it with paint, then roll the brush along the raised part of the tray four to six times. This will evenly coat and distribute the paint on the roller and prevent dripping. You want the roller to be thoroughly saturated with paint (if you can see patches of the roller under the paint, dip it in the well again) but not dripping.

7. Paint a *W* on your wall. This method helps to evenly distribute the paint and to avoid streaks from your roller.

    Tip: Prime the wall first, especially when you are going from a dark wall, like red or dark green, to a light wall, like white or beige.

8. Once the paint has been distributed evenly with the W method, fill in the *W* area by using your roller to paint up and down, and continue until that section of wall is covered with paint. Repeat this process until your first coat is complete.

9. Before doing a second coat, make sure the first coat is dry to the touch. How long this will take depends on what kind of paint you are using. I usually wait about thirty minutes if I'm using a latex paint with an eggshell finish.

    Tip: Interior walls usually need two coats of paint, though depending on a variety of factors like the brand of paint and finish, you might need three. You'll know if you need another coat if the finish is streaky and you can see marks from your paint roller.

HOW TO | Paint with Limewash

I recommend always referring to the directions on the can, but this is the technique that works for me when using pre-mixed limewash paint.

Painting with limewash is a bit different than painting with regular paint because you must add water to it as you go. You also want to make sure you're using a large, wide brush—never a roller. You'll see the brushstrokes, creating a layered pattern that I love, and you can build up the color with multiple coats to get a customized look. The first coat will always look like you've done something terribly wrong to your wall but trust the process! Once the second and third coats dry, it will look like a custom mural.

What Fabric Rollers to Use and When

Shed-resistant: Use with semigloss or high gloss paint so lint doesn't show when applied.

Microfiber and foam: Use for a smooth finish on cabinet doors in a kitchen, or when painting Ikea furniture to make it look as though it was applied with a paint sprayer.

Knit rollers: A good choice for eggshell or flat paint finishes.

WHAT YOU'LL NEED

Limewash paint

Wide paintbrush (usually called a masonry brush)

Drop cloth

Water in a container big enough to fit the brush

INSTRUCTIONS

1. Arrange your paint, brush, drop cloth, and container of water near the wall you're going to paint. Most limewash paints will tell you to mix water into the paint, but I like to keep the water and paint separate.

2. Dip your brush into the paint and then into the water, and paint *X* patterns on the wall. Use more water for a lighter, cloud-like finish and use less if you want the wall to be darker. It's really an intuitive process and completely depends on how you want the wall to look.

3. Let your first coat dry to assess the coverage, and then decide how many more coats to do. I usually use one coat on a wall when I want more texture than color, and three coats when I want a dramatic accent wall with lots of color and texture.

HOW TO

Apply Paint with a Sponge

I think this is hands down one of my most re-created DIYs, and I suspect it's because it's so easy to do but has such a big impact. I used black paint because I wanted it to really pop against the white wall, but you could do any color. This method is guaranteed to look like wallpaper, which is why I love it!

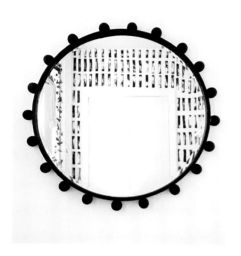

WHAT YOU'LL NEED

Scissors

Melamine sponge

Paint

Small paint tray or container

INSTRUCTIONS

1. Using scissors, cut a melamine sponge into about 4 by 2 inch (10 by 5 cm) rectangles. I found using a regular sponge didn't absorb the paint as well and left a pattern on the wall.

2. Pour paint in a small paint tray or container and dip one of the rectangles into paint.

3. Stamp the paint on your wall with the sponge with an equal distance between each rectangle. You don't have to actually measure the distance; the imperfectness of it is totally a part of the charm!

Pick a desk with a rounded edge so it contrasts the boxiness of your bed.

Dividing a Space Using Paint

One of my favorite ways to use paint is functionally, whether that be with a shape, like an arch, or just a crisp strip of color. If you live in a small, open space with no walls (hello, studio apartments) and are struggling to create zones, a contrasting paint color on the wall will act as a visual divide, even if there isn't a physical one.

In this tiny apartment, the only place to put a desk was beside the bed. Since the tenant was working from home, she needed to make it work. I decided to frame the desk with a dark paint color and carried it all the way to the ceiling. Even though the desk is right beside the bed, the bold streak creates a designated area just for work.

If your desk is beside your bed, set up one side of it as a side table with an alarm clock and reading light.

HOW TO

Get a Straight, Clean, and Crisp Paint Line in the Middle of an Open Wall

Other Ways to Divide a Space with Paint

Paint a semicircle behind your bed to create a faux headboard.

Paint the bottom half of a wall to get a chair rail molding effect without any nails.

If you have a nook in your home, paint it a different color, including any shelves you install. You'll get a built-in look for a fraction of the cost.

Paint an arch to frame art or a mirror.

WHAT YOU'LL NEED

Long level

Pencil

Painter's tape

Paint in the color of your existing wall and in the new color

Small paintbrush

INSTRUCTIONS

1. Decide the size of the area you want painted.

2. Use a long level and a pencil to draw two straight lines from the top of your wall to the bottom, one where the painted area will start and the other where it will end.

3. Stick painter's tape along the outside of both lines you just drew, from the ceiling to the floor.

4. Using a small paintbrush, paint over the inside edge of each strip of painter's tape with the color of your existing wall (*not* the accent wall color!), all the way from the top of the wall to the bottom. This will seal that painter's tape to the wall so that the accent wall color won't be able to bleed underneath the tape and you'll get the crispest line possible!

5. Let it dry, and then go back with your color of choice, painting over the tape and the seal you just painted. When your wall is dry and you pull the tape off, you'll have a super crisp line.

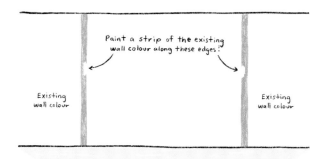

Paint a strip of the existing wall colour along these edges!

Existing wall colour

Existing wall colour

Existing wall colour

Existing wall colour

HOW TO

Install Peel-and-Stick Wallpaper

One of the greatest discoveries in the early days of my decorating career was peel-and-stick wallpaper. Up until then, I associated wallpaper with my grandmother's floral dining room in the British countryside, not with the modern colors and patterns I was seeing in cool, boutique hotels. And on top of adding a ton of style to a room, peel-and-stick wallpaper is renter friendly! I quickly added it into my toolkit of ways to add pattern and color to walls without a permanent commitment. Wallpaper is still one of my favorite ways to decorate a space, and it's also relatively easy to install.

3

4

5

6

WHAT YOU'LL NEED

Peel-and-stick wallpaper

Tape measure

Long level

Pencil

Plastic wallpaper smoothing tool or lint-free cloth

Utility knife

INSTRUCTIONS

1. Measure the wall you want to wallpaper. Lots of wallpaper companies will have a calculator built into their website so you can determine the amount of wallpaper you need. If the company you are using doesn't provide this tool, calculate the wall's square footage by multiplying the wall's width and height (measured in feet and rounded up to the nearest foot). Remember, order a bit extra!

2. Unbox your paper and measure the width of a panel.

3. Using your tape measure, make a mark on the wall as to where the first panel will end, width-wise. Using a level and a pencil, draw a straight line from the top of your wall all the way to the bottom at the mark you just made. Never line up your panels to the ceiling or the edge of the wall, as they're likely not straight. Instead, line up the end of the first panel to the straight line you made as your guide.

4. Line up the first panel with the line you drew and peel the wallpaper backing off bit by bit, top to bottom.

5. Smooth your panel onto the wall with a plastic wallpaper smoothing tool or a lint-free cloth. To make this easier, have another person pull off the back while you smooth.

6. When you reach the top of your baseboard, use the straight edge of your wallpaper smoothing tool (or anything else you can find that's straight, like a credit card) to press the paper into the baseboard so it's easier to cut.

7. Use a utility knife to trim excess wallpaper at the bottom or sides.

8. Continue with the rest of the panels, but this time, line them up to each other by matching the pattern.

Renter Friendly!

HOW TO

Install Peel-and-Stick Decals

If you aren't ready to venture into wallpaper just yet, decals are a great way to get your toes wet! They're substantially less involved to install and are great for small spaces that just need a little pop.

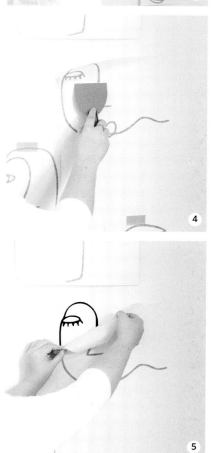

WHAT YOU'LL NEED

Peel-and-stick decals

Soap

Water

Scissors

Painter's tape

Plastic wallpaper smoothing tool or lint-free cloth

INSTRUCTIONS

1. You'll likely receive your decals on one large sheet. Cut them out and leave about a one-inch border. You don't have to worry about being precise.

2. Use a microfiber cloth, soap, and water to clean your wall.

3. Map out where you want the decals to go by taping them to the wall with painter's tape. Move them around until you get your preferred placement.

4. Peel the back off a decal and use a plastic wallpaper smoothing tool or lint-free cloth to stick it on the wall.

5. Slowly peel off the top transfer layer from the decal.

6. Repeat steps 4 and 5 until you have applied all decals.

Styling a Shelf

My favorite kind of shelving is a perfect mix of function and decoration, and when you live in a small space, making use of vertical wall space with shelving is a must. When everything's out in the open, styling is so important. I know styling shelving can be overwhelming, and although some will tell you there are "rules" to follow, think of these tips as a starting point. Be prepared to continuously tweak and step back until you get a combo that feels right.

If you don't have a ton of books to store on your shelving, you can have more fun with decor. If you do have books that need a home, start by organizing those and then start bringing in your decor.

A List of Decor Ideas to Layer in Your Shelf

Picture frames with personal/family photos

Small plants like succulents or cacti

Decorative baskets for storage

Vases (They don't have to have anything in them! Make sure they're a variety of heights.)

Candles

Bowls (Look for interesting shapes and materials, like a wavy wooden bowl.)

Ceramic knotted decor

Strings of beads

Table clocks

A. **Mix it up:** Vary the way books are displayed. Stand them up and stack them horizontally, but also stack them in piles on each shelf to break up the shelving visually. Place tiny trinkets like succulents on top of a stack to add decoration.

B. **Add storage:** Layer in decorative baskets to create storage and hide clutter. (Have fun with embellishments like pom-poms!)

C. **Shelving isn't just for books:** Put things like shoes on display if you are lacking closet space.

D. **Add ambient lighting:** Add a battery-powered table lamp for decoration and to create a mood. For a plug-in light, you can drill a hole in the back of your shelf to feed the cord through and hide it.

E. **Three is the magic number:** When adding decor, cluster things in groups of three in similar colors. This is the key to making your shelf look styled and unified, instead of cluttered.

F. **Don't forget about height:** Adding a variety of heights through both stacks of books and trinkets will keep your shelf looking dynamic.

G. **Keep colors balanced:** Spread hues throughout all the shelves to keep your eyes moving across the whole unit. Don't place all the red items on one shelf, for example, unless you're going for a rainbow effect!

Arrange, step back, arrange again: You likely won't get the perfect arrangement the first time, and that's okay!

Layering is the secret to making your shelf look styled.

M IS AN OFFICE & OTHER

M

MY TINY ATLAS

SHEARER & TEPLIN   THE HOME EDIT

Magnolia Table   VOLUME 2   JOANNA GAINES

IGN DILEMMAS   Joanna Thornhill

lista

NATHAN

Place a piece of art on a shelf and stack books or decor in front of it to make your shelf look full.

feels like

All About Art

HERE'S THE THING ABOUT ART: IT'S THE PERFECT WAY

to accentuate your style, bring color or texture into your space, and fill empty corners of your home. For me, displaying art I love always makes my space feel like *mine*. I'll never forget the first piece of art I bought in my early twenties. It was a bright yellow screen print of three women sunbathing in retro bathing suits by Toronto artist Stephanie Cheng that cost me less than fifty dollars. I purchased it directly from her at a decor show, bought a frame for it, and hung it at the top of the stairs at my parents' home. I remember being so excited by how much I loved the piece, and how happy that tiny corner made me. For a long time, I found purchasing art for my home intimidating, and it took me awhile to discover what kinds of pieces I wanted hanging on my walls. I quickly began to realize that you don't have to go to art auctions or buy multi-thousand-dollar pieces to be someone who can have art hanging in your home. Buying Stephanie's piece was the first time I had purchased a piece of art simply because I loved it, and I haven't strayed from that mentality since.

Buying Art: Where to Start

Whenever I'm planning a room and don't have a ton of budget to spend on art and accessories (which is usually always!), I turn to places like Etsy or other online art markets where independent artists sell their work or have sold the rights for a specific piece to be reproduced and sold in mass quantities. These kinds of art market prices are generally more accessible simply because tens of thousands of the same poster exist. They're a great starting point to get a sense of what you are drawn to because they have just about every medium to browse, such as photography, illustration, and paintings.

When I'm making over other people's spaces, art is usually something I think about near the end of the design plan once I've got a clear color palette and style nailed down. I tend to gravitate toward budget-friendly art options, which I go over in more detail below, as investing in art pieces is such a personal purchase.

Have a brick wall? Attach your art to it using brick clips, which hook on to the top and bottom of the brick.

Places I Love to Purchase Reproductions and Posters

Minted: A market of independent artists who receive ongoing commission. I love Minted because you can browse by medium, and they have beautiful framing options as well. Minted's collection is carefully selected and curated.

Society6: An open community of artists from around the world. I love Society6 for the variation of art sold. Anyone can sell their work, so there are thousands of pieces to choose from.

Juniper Print Shop: An online shop selling art that can be downloaded and then printed to fit most standard-size frames. It's great for finding oversized pieces if you have a large, blank wall to be filled.

My online store, Pom'd Marketplace: I work with local artists I admire to design digital downloadable art prints that are sold on my website at an affordable price.

What I love about poster art is that it can be easily swapped in and out of frames and changed often. Because of this, I usually put these pieces in inexpensive frames that have clips on the back, so I can swap out art wherever I feel like it.

Places I Love to Purchase Original Art

Directly from the artist: One of the ways I discover new artists is by browsing decor magazines, books, and online. I love following artists digitally because I feel connected to their process.

Etsy: A platform where artists can sell their work to consumers directly and run their own store. There are also lots of artists who will do custom pieces, if you have something personal or specific in mind.

Instagram: If there's a piece that you spot in a photo of someone's room on Instagram, chances are they've tagged the artist. If not, ask them where it's from!

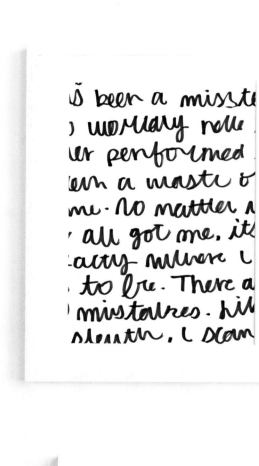

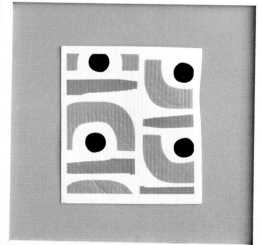

Where to Find Large Pieces on a Budget

I tend to get original, more expensive artwork professionally framed. Framing art is not inexpensive (upward of one hundred dollars, depending on the size of your piece), but it's the best way to preserve and protect work for a long time. I frame pieces that I know I'm going to have in many homes to come.

In my own home, I've slowly started collecting original, one-of-a-kind pieces that come at a higher price point because the artist has created a limited-edition work that is numbered and signed. When I'm buying these kinds of pieces, I am not trying to fit them into my current design style, but instead purchasing pieces that I really love. If you are concerned about the artwork in your home matching the rest of your pieces, try pulling out colors from the piece and weaving those colors through your accessories, like rugs and throw cushions.

Rentable art: Some galleries and marketplaces will rent out their art. It's a great way to both try before you buy and change up the art in your home constantly. Renting art makes high-end, original pieces accessible to more people.

Printable artwork: Some artists will sell their prints as downloadable files at a fraction of the cost. You can print it on your home printer or have it professionally blown up into an oversized print.

Wallpaper and gift wrap: Throw a piece of beautiful wallpaper or gift wrap into an oversized frame to create a bold statement for a fraction of the cost of original art.

Art That Isn't Framed

I get *tons* of questions on what to do with a blank wall. You know the ones—empty and seemingly full of possibilities yet somehow the hardest to fill. Sometimes an expansive blank wall calls for the unexpected. Here are some items you maybe haven't considered throwing on your wall that will make an impact:

Wood wall art: Find something in an interesting shape, like the piece by Katie Gong on page 108. Or forage your own piece of driftwood and hang it for a rustic look.

Rugs or blankets: Bring on the texture and color by hanging a beautiful piece like the one on page 108 on your wall. Depending on the size of the rug, you can usually just attach it to the wall with a couple of nails. Note: Rugs are usually so heavy that using nails is the best way to make sure they stay safely in place, so this might not be the most renter-friendly option!

Dried floral arrangements: Lots of floral shops will sell dried arrangements like the one on page 109 and can customize the colors if custom made. Bonus: They stay fresh forever!

Wall hangings: There are so many talented artists that create wall hangings out of macramé, thread, and yarn.

Wood wall art

Rugs or Blankets

Dried Floral
Arrangement

Wall Hanging

Gallery Wall Tips

I love a minimal, symmetrical gallery wall *but* those can get pricey. Instead, my go-to for gallery walls is usually to create a more eclectic, casual display of things that I have collected, whether it be art prints, notes, cards, or photographs. The best part about this kind of gallery wall is that you likely already have everything you need right at home to create a fun display.

A. **Old Post-it notes:** Sweet messages left on the fridge make cute, sentimental art pieces. Make sure you frame the note with a mat to make notes, cards, and other smaller items look polished. If your piece is an unusual size, you can order custom mats online—going into a professional framing store not necessary!

B. **Wrapping paper:** Have a little left behind from a birthday? The fun patterns and colors make for great abstract pieces. Keep the creases of the paper to add texture and interest to your wall.

C. **Your favorite song:** Handwrite your favorite lyric or quote on paper. Keep it messy to create an abstract piece.

D. **Wallpaper:** Like wrapping paper, wallpaper is a great thing to frame for a hit of bold pattern and color. Order sample swatches or keep leftovers to frame.

E. **Sentimental blooms:** Create a keepsake out of your birthday or anniversary florals by hanging them on your wall. Dry and press them in a book for a few days before you frame.

F. **Affirmation cards:** Not only are affirmation cards (which you can buy pre-made from small artists or shops) usually quite pretty, they're also a fun way to keep the positive words flowing. Stick them up with decorative washi tape and change them every day.

G. **Old greeting cards:** It feels weird to toss these, right? Don't! Small, local artists sometimes turn their prints into cards.

H. **Tea towels:** Ever come across a tea towel that looked too cute to use? Frame it! Look for something with either texture, pattern, or color (or all three!) to make a statement. Cuts of fabric also work!

I. **Pantone cards or paint chips:** Create a collage of color or hang the individual swatches on your wall. These look cute hung up with washi tape.

J. **Dishcloths:** The pattern and texture of cloths create great visual interest. Swedish dishcloths tend to have great patterns!

K. **Cane webbing:** If you have some of this material leftover from a project, pop it into a frame and let the natural texture of it shine. Paint it a fun color to match the rest of your gallery wall.

L. **Squares of canvas:** Cut canvas into squares and paint them using leftover interior paint to match the rest of your home. Not all art has to be hung. Lean big prints against the wall.

Use colored paper as a backdrop for the smaller pieces like cards and dried florals. This will add color and make these tinier pieces pop.

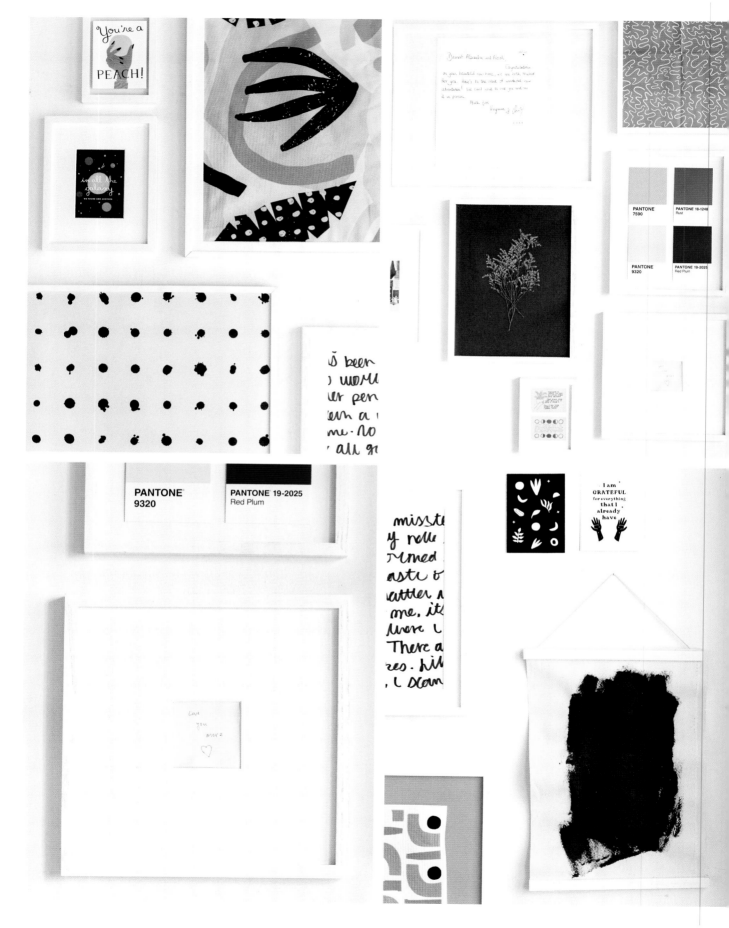

Renter-Friendly Ways to Hang Art
If You Can't Put Holes in the Wall

Adhesive hanging strips. Before you buy, make sure you check the weight that the strips can hold to ensure they will support the item you are hanging.

Washi tape (a decorative tape made from rice paper). This is a fun way to hang lightweight posters or prints, and also a fun way to make frames! It comes in different colors and patterns and can be found at most craft or paper stores.

Wooden poster hangers, which can be hung using an adhesive hook.

Heavy-duty double-sided adhesive tape.

Display art in groups on the floor, leaning up against the wall for a casual (but still styled) look.

Keep It Bright
with Lighting

AS YOU MAY HAVE NOTICED THROUGHOUT THIS BOOK,

I have a love affair with lighting. It's the perfect way to accessorize a room and bring in style, texture, and color with one piece. Before I started working in design, I viewed lights in a home as a permanent fixture—once it's in the wall, it's there to stay unless you rewire your whole home, right? Wrong! There is, of course, hardwiring involved, but it's not as scary or time-consuming as you may think.

In a lot of my makeovers, switching out lighting is the change I look forward to the most when making over a space, because it's one of the easiest and most impactful ways to add personality. When I'm starting my design plan and moodboarding, I'm always looking at lights as the hero pieces of the space—I'm someone who goes big and statement-worthy with my lighting. The other thing I love about lighting, beyond the way it looks, is how it makes me *feel*, and I find that details even down to the temperature of a lightbulb can affect this. A room will always look instantly cozier with a table lamp turned on in the evening. Equally, there's nothing worse than when the only source of light in a room is an overhead light that casts a cold, bluish hue. Those who have lived with me know that I have the unconscious habit of walking through my home and turning off all the overhead lighting while simultaneously switching on all the table lamps. I can't feel fully at home or relaxed until I do.

HOW TO | Hardwire a Light

Below, I've provided a step-by-step guide to hardwiring a light yourself. Just check that it's legal to do so where you live—in some countries, hiring an electrician to change out lights is required by law. As with any DIY project, use your discretion. If you don't feel comfortable rewiring a light by yourself (I completely understand), hiring an electrician from a service like TaskRabbit or Angi is inexpensive and quick.

WHAT YOU'LL NEED

Voltage tester pen (optional)

Screwdriver

Colored twist-on wire connectors

Electrical tape

INSTRUCTIONS

1. Before doing any electrical work, turn off all power to that area of the home using your circuit breaker. To be extra safe, use a voltage tester pen to check if there's any live power in your light fixture once the circuit breaker has been turned off. You can find these for under ten dollars at the hardware store, and they're worth investing in only if you feel as if you are going to be changing lights out yourself. Once that's done, remove the light one wire at a time.

2. Secure the light bracket to the electrical box in the ceiling using the screwdriver. This bracket comes with the light.

3. Take your ground wire from the electrical box and hold it parallel to the ground wire in the pendant light, with the ends of the wires aligned. Twist a twist-on wire connector over the ends of the wires to hold them together. Screw the twist-on wire connector over the two wires until you feel resistance, to ensure the wires are secure and will not fall out of the twist-on wire connector. Twist-on wire connectors are for one-time use, so don't reuse from the old fixture!

4. Repeat step 3 for the live and neutral wires. Pair live with live, neutral with neutral, and use a twist-on wire connector to secure each pair. If there are any extra wires outside of the three we've discussed in this section, just cap them off with a twist-on wire connector.

5. Wrap electrical tape at the base of each twist-on wire connector. This will ensure the twist-on wire connector stays on and that no metal or debris gets into the twist-on wire connector.

6. Gently coax all the wires into the electrical box.

7. Fasten the pendant light cover plate onto the bracket that you screwed into the electrical box in step 2.

This is what you'll find when you take your old light down. In the ceiling, there will be an electrical box. Inside the box there will be a green or bare copper wire (the grounding wire), a black wire (the live wire), and a white wire (the neutral wire). If your wires are a different color, labels should be on the wires to indicate if they are live, grounding, or neutral.

A. Electrical tape
B. Electrical box
C. Twist-on wire connector
D. Screwdriver
E. Voltage pen
F. Faceplate
G. Bracket

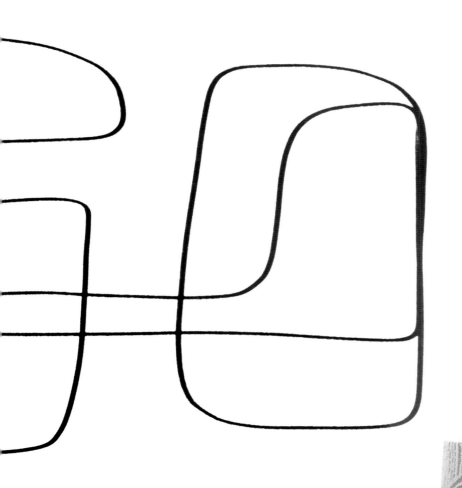

Psst *If you have a light with an exposed bulb, opt for a decorative one. From ones with embellished glass to exposed filaments called Edison bulbs, there are tons of options.*

RECIPES FOR WHOLE FOOD, GRAIN-FREE DESSERTS

JENNA RAE CAKES AND SWEET TREATS

MANDY'S GOURMET SALADS

Bulb Temperature Guide

If you've ever stood in the lightbulb section of the hardware store, you've probably wondered why there are so many. I've asked the same question! But I also understand the impact of the temperature of lighting. There's no point in having a stunning pendant light with a bulb temperature that's too cold or too warm. I've always been amazed at the impact that lighting has on me. I find bright, bluish, daytime lighting really cold, sometimes to the detriment of my mood. I instead prefer soft, warm bulbs—they truly make a space feel cozy. Here's a guide you can bring into the hardware store with you so you're not staring sightlessly at all the bulbs in front of you.

First, let's break down what's on the lightbulb box.

There are three key decorative-related things you should look out for on the box when purchasing a lightbulb: the kind of bulb (LED, incandescent, halogen, or compact fluorescent), the number of lumens (how much light the bulb will give off), and the number of kelvins (how warm or cool the light is).

The number of lumens you need depends on how big your space is. There's a mathematical equation you can do to figure out the exact lumens you need in your space based on its size.

First, you want to measure your room and calculate its square footage. Then, you want to refer to the chart on page 120 and determine how many foot-candles (a unit of measurement that determines the amount of brightness you need per square foot) are recommended for that particular room. Multiply the two numbers together and you'll have the total amount of lumens your room will need. For example, if you have a 100 square foot living room, refer to the chart to see that 10 foot-candles is the recommended starting point for a living room; then multiply 100 by 10 and you get 1,000, which is the amount of lumens you'll need.

For larger spaces, one lightbulb usually won't give you all the lumens you need for the space, which is why it's important to layer in different sources of lighting like pendants, floor lamps, table lamps, and sconces, especially if your room is on the larger side.

Psst *Don't have a dimmer switch? You can still have lighting that dims! Smart lightbulbs will connect to your phone and allow you to control the color and brightness of your bulb at any time. You can even set your lights on timers if you have a smart home device, so they'll turn on or off automatically at the times you set.*

Room and Foot-Candles Needed

Living room	10–20
Kitchen	30–40
Dining room	30–40
Bedroom	10–20
Hallway	5–10
Bathroom	70–80

Note: When determining how many foot-candles you'll need, I recommend starting on the lower end of the range provided and working your way up if you need more light. It's always easier to add lighting if you need more! The temperature of the light that your bulb gives off is measured in Kelvins. Choosing the number is a personal decision, as it's mostly an aesthetic choice, depending on if you want a warmer hue in your space or one that's more of a truer white. Bring the illustration below to the hardware store to reference, but note that a lot of lighting packages will also include a scale like this.

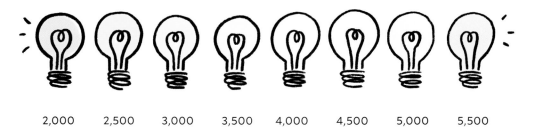

| 2,000 | 2,500 | 3,000 | 3,500 | 4,000 | 4,500 | 5,000 | 5,500 |

Snap and bring with you to shop!

Psst *When purchasing a bulb, you'll likely want to go for an LED. LEDs are much more energy-efficient but look similar to incandescent bulbs—the difference being that they last years longer.*

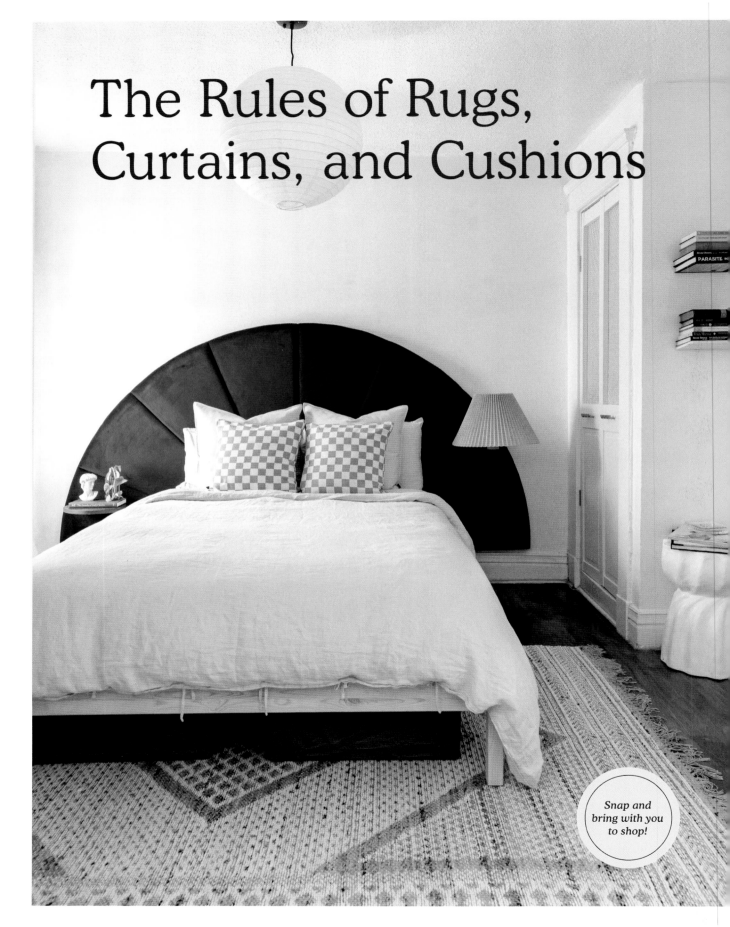

The Rules of Rugs, Curtains, and Cushions

Snap and bring with you to shop!

THE POWER OF ACCESSORIES IN DESIGN IS UNMATCHED.

In a lot of ways, they are the items that anchor the style of your space and give you the ability to change the look and feel of your more permanent furniture pieces. You'll see the countless ways I've used accessories in makeovers to bring spaces to life in Part 3, but this is more about the rules that are crucial to follow when selecting the sizes of these pieces. One of the things I found most intimidating about decorating when I first started was navigating all the rules that came with accessories. Does all my living room furniture need to sit on top of my rug? What about cushions—how many is *too many* on a sofa? And how much fabric from my curtains can be draping onto my floor?

One thing I've always tried to steer away from in my makeovers, and throughout this book, is being strict when it comes to rules of design. However, when it comes to rugs, curtains, and cushions, there are some general size, length, and combination rules I like to follow. I'd like to make it known that these rules took me a long time to get right, and it's only looking back at my makeovers that I've realized in this instance, following certain guidelines means a more intentional-looking, styled, and polished space.

Rugs

The size of a rug in a room has to be just right, or else it completely ruins the look of the space for me. A rug that is too small makes the room feel drastically smaller than it actually is, while a rug that is too big and hitting the sides of your walls is an obvious indication that you didn't measure the space and purchased the wrong size of rug. Use this guide when picking a rug for each of these rooms so you land on a size that is just right.

The living room: Your rug should be big enough so that the front legs of your sofa sit on the rug while the rug also fills the rest of your room. You don't want it hitting the baseboards, but you don't want it stopping in the middle of your living room, either. If you have lounge chairs, those should sit comfortably with all legs on top of the rug as well. If your rug goes underneath your media unit, it's too big. Instead, it should hit the sweet spot of stopping just in front.

The bedroom: A rug will instantly up the cozy factor, but make sure it's large enough. Your entire bed frame (and nightstands) can sit on the area rug, or the rug can clear your nightstands and begin lower down the bedframe. Either way, always make sure at least two or all four legs of your bed sit on the rug. If it's floating in front of your bed, it's too small!

The dining room: If you have a rug in your dining room, all of your furniture should sit comfortably on it, including your chairs when they are pulled out from under the table. You don't want guests pulling back their chairs and having the back legs fall off the rug or trying to scoot in and having the legs get caught!

Psst I often will use my digital floor plan to determine the size of rug I need in every makeover I do—it's a great way to visualize if a rug will be too small or too big.

Curtains

Even after completing more than one hundred makeovers, whenever I replace curtains that are too short, it's like something magical has occurred. Suddenly the space looks taller, more styled and pulled-together. Short curtains are similar to wearing pants that don't fit because they are noticeably too short—and not in a cute way.

Sometimes when I install curtains, I like them to just hit the floor. This gives your space a more formal, crisp look, similar to a perfect, tailored pant that hits your ankle. Most times, however, I like to pool about 2 to 3 inches (5 to 7.5 cm) of fabric on the floor to give a more relaxed feel, and I find this looks best with curtains made from linen. If you're unsure about what length to order, always opt for the longer size. You can always hem your curtains with iron-on tape.

I was once told that the goal when installing curtain rods shouldn't be to hide your windows but instead to frame them, and that's stuck with me ever since. If you have the space, your curtain rod should be hung two-thirds of the distance between your window and ceiling—that means it should sit closer to the ceiling, not the window frame. About 4 to 6 inches (10 to 15 cm) should usually do the trick. This will draw your eye up and make your ceilings appear way taller than they actually are. Trust me when I say this trick works: I've done it in countless small spaces, and it's magic every time. If your ceiling isn't tall enough for the two-thirds rule of thumb, hang the rod as close to the ceiling as possible, under the crown molding if there is any. If you have the room, your curtain rod should extend 8 to 12 inches (20 to 30.5 cm) on either side of your window frame to make it appear wider; this is trickier to accomplish in a small space. If this doesn't work in your space, opt for the widest amount possible, while making sure the finial (that's the end cap of your rod) still fits and isn't butting against the wall.

I've often found that people think having a small window means using less curtain fabric, but I've found that's not the case. One curtain panel will make your window look smaller and unfinished. Two panels creates a more finished look.

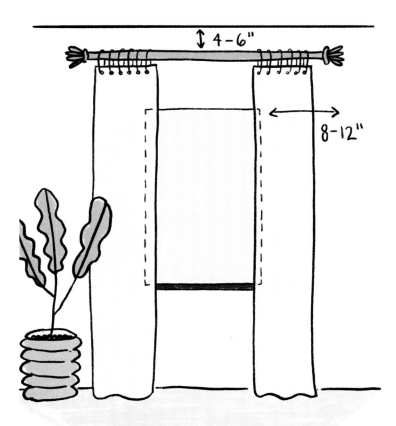

4–6"

8–12"

Psst *Avoid hanging your curtain rod directly on your window frame (unless you absolutely have to). This will make your window (and space in general) seem really small.*

Psst *Picking accessories can be overwhelming. I always find it easiest to start with a rug that I like and then create a color scheme by using hues from that piece and weaving them throughout the rest of the space in my curtains, cushions, and styling pieces.*

For the square cushions, alternate between sizes 22 × 22 inches and 20 × 20 inches for varying heights

One Sofa Four Ways: The Power of Accessories

Okay, so you've got all the rules nailed down, but now how do you actually style all these pieces together? Here is one sofa outfitted four ways, with different rugs and cushion combinations. It's amazing how just swapping out these two things can drastically change the way your space looks.

Snap and bring with you to shop!

My Go-to Throw Cushion Formula for Sofas

Two solid-colored cushions, one big and one small
+
A small cushion (not square) with pattern or texture
+
A square cushion with a pattern
+
A square, textured cushion with a pattern
+
A smaller, lumbar cushion that's patterned or textured

LOOK 1:
Airy and neutral

Low, wood sofa legs, textured white rug, terra-cotta-colored cushions, raffia materials

LOOK 2:
Bold and colorful

Gold sofa legs, colorful rug, orange and blue cushions, hits of creams and whites

Pull colors from your rug into your cushion covers.

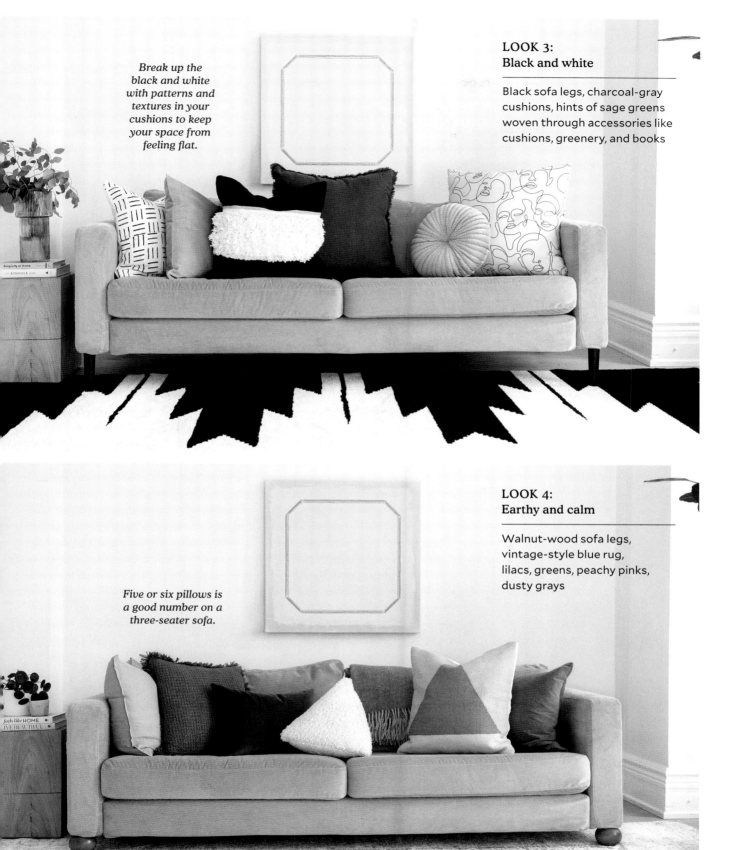

Break up the black and white with patterns and textures in your cushions to keep your space from feeling flat.

LOOK 3:
Black and white

Black sofa legs, charcoal-gray cushions, hints of sage greens woven through accessories like cushions, greenery, and books

Five or six pillows is a good number on a three-seater sofa.

LOOK 4:
Earthy and calm

Walnut-wood sofa legs, vintage-style blue rug, lilacs, greens, peachy pinks, dusty grays

Everything You Need to Know about Hacking Ikea Furniture

SOME OF MY FAVORITE DIY PROJECTS ARE WHEN I GET to hack existing pieces of Ikea furniture. Beyond paint, there are *so many* fronts that companies sell for just about any piece of Ikea furniture to make it look custom and elevated. It's a great way to turn functional pieces into stylish, personalized items that complement your home's style.

Easiest way to update an Ikea nightstand: Replace the fronts with something custom, add decorative knobs, and voilà! A new, elevated piece.

Companies That Hack Ikea Furniture

Norse Interiors: Custom fronts for Ikea storage like sideboards, media consoles, dressers, and nightstands in colors that match existing Ikea pieces for a seamless upgrade.

A. S. Helsingö: Kitchen, wardrobe, and sideboard fronts for Ikea pieces in stunning, soft, muted colors ranging from sage greens to dusty pinks. Their products are rooted in Scandinavian design and created by designers, architects, and artists.

Semihandmade: A huge selection of doors for Ikea kitchen, bathroom, and media console cabinets. You'll be amazed at how personalized you can make an Ikea kitchen look!

Superfront: In addition to other things, this company has amazing custom wardrobe doors for the Ikea Pax system. They also sell end panels if you want to change the sides of your Pax unit as well.

Nieu Cabinet Doors: Sells custom cabinet doors for Ikea kitchens and wardrobes. They also sell raw MDF cabinet fronts, so you can paint them any color you'd like.

HOW TO

Paint Ikea Furniture
That Has a Laminate Finish

If you've ever tried painting over furniture that has a glossy topcoat, you know that it's basically impossible to get an even finish, let alone get it to stick, if you're not using the right materials and tools. But it is possible with the right prep—and a really easy way to customize furniture and make it your own.

WHAT YOU'LL NEED

Medium-grit sandpaper (anything between 120–220 grit) or electric sander

Lint-free cloth

Two foam rollers

High-adhesion, shellac-based primer

Paint (in an oil-based, eggshell finish)

INSTRUCTIONS

1. Sand off the glossy top layer using the medium-grit sandpaper or electric sander.

2. Thoroughly wipe off all the dust with a dry, lint-free cloth.

3. Use a foam roller to paint on a high-adhesion primer that sticks to laminate. A primer with shellac in it is recommended because it sticks well to tricky surfaces and hardens to a durable finish. The instructions for the primer you are using may say that you can use this primer without sanding first, but I always recommend sanding for a smooth finish. Wait for the primer to dry before moving on to the next step.

4. Use a new foam roller to paint on the color of your choice. I reccomend always using an oil-based paint because it's much more durable for surfaces that will see lots of traffic, like a shoe cabinet or coffee table. Make sure to follow the instructions on the can as the process differs from latex paint application.

5. Let it dry and cure overnight so the paint hardens. This will reduce the risk of lifting.

Psst *Learn how to hack your Ikea* sofa on page 198.

Beautiful Alternatives

Over the years, I've seen *a lot* of decor products, and although there's nothing like a gorgeous velvet sofa to get my heart beating in excitement, the items I'm always most excited about are the small everyday accessories that have a big impact or just bring a tiny bit of joy every time I use them.

I call these items "beautiful alternatives": everyday items that you didn't know could be cute, but are game changers for your space. You may not have the budget for a brand-new kitchen makeover, but some beautiful alternatives to those standard kitchen items will make your space feel like new.

When I moved into my first apartment, I vowed that everything would be cute and got rid of anything that didn't bring me joy, à la Marie Kondo. I even tossed the toilet brush, challenging myself to find something decorative that I would love to look at every time I walked into my bathroom. Here is a selection from my ever-growing list of things you likely haven't even realized there's a beautiful alternative for:

Dish rack

Dishcloths

Dish brush

Broom

Garden hose

Step ladder

Garbage can

Salt and pepper shakers

S-hook for ceiling light

Reusable straws

Clothing hangers

Wall hooks

Trivets

Exposed lightbulbs

PART

3 | Real Rooms

No one knows this, but on the second day of my internship at *Chatelaine* I almost didn't go. As in, I almost threw in the towel and quit. I felt way in over my head, and nowhere near qualified enough to even be *interning* at a publication like this one. Being in a room filled with such smart women was intimidating, and I didn't know if I fit into a world that I really knew nothing about. In short, I was terrified.

That feeling never really faded, and if anything, only increased as my role changed and grew. I'll never forget the week after I launched the second *Home Primp* episode. I was so proud of the five-minute video, where I walked viewers through how I transformed my bedroom bookshelves, which were mismatched laminate wood (one dark, one light), their shelves bending under the weight of being stuffed to the brim with books and trinkets. It was my first *real* DIY project. I adorned the back of the shelves with wallpaper in a black-and-white dotted print and decked it out with cute pom-pom baskets for storage. This video landed me a segment on morning television (the memory of me hauling my entire book collection, along with three bookshelves, into the downtown Toronto television studio is hilarious to think about now), and though fairly simple in principle, it was the first time I had seen a vision in my head come to life.

During this time, as things really started to change for me and new opportunities like being on television began to arise, I became increasingly nervous. I was feeling something beyond imposter syndrome. Sometimes, on the really bad days, I felt ashamed and embarrassed to name my achievements out loud. When people asked me what I did for a living, I'd sheepishly say that I was the home editor at *Chatelaine* and at the same time kind of laugh it off. It sounded like a joke in my head, and so saying it out loud did, too.

It didn't help to realize that people who had been in the industry for years before me weren't very receptive to change. Targeting a younger audience at a publication that had catered to a specific subset of women meant that the way we were producing content and the kinds of things we were creating had to change as well. I will *never* forget what one editor at *Chatelaine* said to me as I sat across from her, snot dripping down my face after reading a series of meanspirited comments from women in my industry on that bookshelf video I was so proud of: *In a few years, you'll be talking about this day on a podcast or on a panel somewhere and you'll laugh about it.*

I didn't believe it then, and it's still hard for me to wrap my mind around the fact that I'm writing about that in this book—*my book.*

My point is, change is hard. Having confidence is hard. Taking yourself seriously, especially when you're taking a different road than those who came before you, is hard. But that day, I remember giving myself an ultimatum. I could throw in the towel like I almost did on day two of my internship and leave the world of home decor to the editors who had known it so well before me. Or I could tell myself over and over again that there's a space for them and the work they do, and there's a space for me, too, and both spaces can exist at the same time.

I chose the latter, and in a lot of ways that day shaped my career. It made me even *more* certain that someone needed to create a space in the world of home decor for renters and first-time homeowners who didn't have oodles of money to spend on the items adorning the spreads of glossy magazines.

I knew for certain when I started writing this book that I wanted a section where I broke down exactly how I made each space come to life, to make the world of design and home decor feel a lot more approachable. A lot of the time when you pick up a coffee-table book like this one, it's filled with picture-perfect spaces that feel aspirational, rather than attainable—kind of like how I felt when I read all those comments from those editors. But the goal of this section is to break down exactly how I transformed each space so you feel empowered to create a room of your own and carve out an area for yourself to feel truly proud of.

The Kitchen

THE THOUGHT OF
making over your kitchen is likely
terrifying, which makes sense. When
you open *any* home decor magazine or
coffee-table book, you're usually faced
with gorgeous kitchens outfitted with
built-in custom cabinetry, shiny new
appliances, and gorgeous tiled flooring.
These spaces are beautiful, but that's
also because kitchen renos are wildly
expensive.

Kitchens, like bathrooms (which we'll
get to later), are daunting spaces to make
over, but they've slowly turned into some
of my favorite rooms to tackle because
the payoff is *big*.

My goal of this section is to break
down the scary aspects of any kitchen
makeover—old laminate countertops,
outdated backsplash tile that can't be
removed, and dark cabinetry that you
could only dream of being white and
bright—and show you how to solve these
things on a budget, DIY style.

Megan's Kitchen

W hen I saw Megan's kitchen, I was struck by how many rentals I've seen like hers: the outdated orange wooden cabinets and laminate countertops that were the same color I had seen at least a hundred times. I loved this makeover because it was *so simple* to transform and turn this kitchen into a retro-inspired dream. Here's how I made it happen.

BEFORE

A. In a small kitchen, go bold with the color. It'll add so much personality to your tiny space.

B. When stuck with larger fixtures like countertops and flooring that can't be replaced, make the outdated colors of your countertops and floor tile work by picking a color for your cabinets that complements them.

C. Put cookbooks on display and within easy reach using a photo ledge.

D. Add a small rug or runner that pulls similar colors from the existing countertops and floor tiles—it'll make them look more intentional.

E. If you have a cabinet that has glass or is open, reserve it for pretty dishware and food in glass jars to create stylish functionality.

HOW TO

Install Peel-and-Stick Backsplash Tiles

Peel-and-stick backsplash tiles for rental kitchens is one of the ultimate game changers because it's completely reversible, is easy to install (like, really easy), and hides just about any ugly, outdated tile. These products allow you to dip your toe into the world of color and pattern without the commitment. You don't need many tools or an adhesive—or even much time—to install it.

1

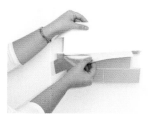

2

3

4

5

WHAT YOU'LL NEED

Long level

Pencil

Utility knife or scissors
(you can use whichever you prefer, but a utility knife will give you a more precise cut)

INSTRUCTIONS

1. Line up your tile to the top of the wall or the bottom of the cabinet. If your wall isn't level (and most of them aren't!), use a long level and a pencil to draw a straight line across.

2. Peel the backing off a tile. You can install peel-and-stick tiles over any kind of tile, and the backsplash you pick doesn't even have to be the same dimensions as the existing tile. Warped, uneven tile will be more difficult to cover, but not impossible.

3. Align the top of the tile to the top of the pencil line and stick it to the wall or tile.

4. Use the grout line on the tile as a guide to stick the next tile, and so on.

5. Use a utility knife with a ruler to trim any edges. You can also use scissors to trim.

Snap and bring with you to shop!

My Favorite Places to Shop for Peel-and-Stick Backsplash

Quadrostyle: Quadrostyle sells sheets of vinyl backsplash in tons of patterns and colors.

Smart Tiles: You can find Smart Tiles at many hardware stores, and they come in lots of traditional styles such as subway, penny, and herringbone.

WallPops: WallPops sells backsplash by the panel, tile, and roll.

Psst — When you're ready to move out of your rental and need to take the tile down, use a hair dryer to warm up the tile's sticky adhesive and then slowly peel it back.

Renter Friendly!

The secret to making any peel-and-stick tile look real is to caulk around the perimeter of the tile. Plus, this will also hide any imperfections or imperfect cuts made when installing. But note, it will make the tiles more permanent.

There are two different types of peel-and-stick tiles I like to use:

Tiled backsplash: This product comes in sheets of tile about 24 by 48 inches (61 by 122 cm) and is installed by lining up the grout lines. The grout lines are indented, making it look realistic. Tiled backsplash is usually a glossy material and feels like tile to the touch. There are tons of realistic classic tile options in this style, like penny, subway, and hexagon-shaped tile.

Vinyl wallpaper backsplash: This product comes in a single long sheet similar to wallpaper except that it's waterproof and meant for high-traffic, water-prone areas like kitchens and bathrooms. Unlike tiled backsplash, the grout lines between tiles are printed on the vinyl, so there are no grooves, which makes it look less realistic. This is a good option if you're looking for patterned tile.

Alexandra's Kitchen

When Noah and I toured our current apartment, I asked our landlords right away if they would be open to me updating the kitchen. I loved the stone countertops and island in the middle of the space, but the backsplash was green and outdated, and the color of the cabinets wasn't super inspiring. This makeover was a larger undertaking than most, but because it was my own space I had the time and flexibility to do a lot more than I typically would.

BEFORE

A. Consider removing upper cabinets if you're craving more light and can sacrifice removing closed storage. It will make your kitchen feel more spacious, and give you a place to put your prettiest dishware on show.

B. If you don't want to paint your cabinet fronts, and your existing cabinet system is from Ikea (you can check this by looking for a sticker on the inside of one of the doors), it's easy to find something that feels custom. A lot of companies sell cabinet fronts for Ikea products and all you need to do is install them. (See page 131 for a list of companies that sell parts that work with Ikea pieces.)

C. Fun fact: You can tile over existing tile!

D. If you want to go with an interesting pattern or color but are afraid of it becoming outdated, try going for an organic shape to add interest.

E. Replacing a standard mounted sink faucet for one that includes a pull-down sprayer head will up your kitchen functionality.

F. Bar stools are a great way to add style to your kitchen. If your bar stools have upholstered seats, consider switching up the fabric for a new look.

HOW TO | Make a Simmer Pot

Scent is a huge part of my home because it's the way I feel calm and grounded in my space. For me, there is such a ritual surrounding having a clean, tidy home and lighting a candle or diffusing essential oils at the end of the workday.

When I was growing up, my mum would make simmer pots in the colder months, and they made our home smell like a cold walk in the woods—the smell of fir trees and crisp, winter air. I've since carried on that tradition when the weather gets cold, and I have so much fun experimenting with different ingredients.

WHAT YOU'LL NEED

Medium pot

Water

Aromatic ingredients like fruits, herbs, and spices

Snap and bring with you to shop!

INSTRUCTIONS

To make a simmer pot, start by boiling a pot of water on the stove. Throw in your selection of ingredients and lower the heat to maintain a simmer. Leave it on your stove for about an hour—set a timer so you don't forget about it!

The ingredients you include are entirely up to you, depending on if you want a sweet-smelling profile or more spicy. Here are my go-to recipes. The amount of each ingredient is just a starting point; how much you use is up to you. Whatever you add more of will create the dominant scent. For these pots, you want the freshest ingredients you can find for the strongest scents possible—nothing dried, unless noted!

Simmer pots last up to about four days, depending on how much fresh fruit you are using. Simply cover it when you're done simmering and top up the water when you go to use it again.

AUTUMN SIMMER POT

Is there anything more autumnal than your home smelling like apple pie?

3 cinnamon sticks
Peel of 2 apples
Peel of 1 orange
A handful of whole cloves

WINTER SIMMER POT

Whenever my mum has this simmering on the stove, I know it's December and probably snowing outside. Lemon and orange give it a fresh uplifting scent, while warm, comforting allspice grounds it.

1 lemon, sliced
1 orange, sliced
1 fig, sliced
3 cinnamon sticks
A few sprigs fresh eucalyptus
A handful of rosemary
Whole cloves
Sliced ginger

SPRING SIMMER POT

The flowers are starting to bloom outside, so bring them inside, too. I love how this simmer pot reminds me that sunshine and warm weather is just around the corner.

1 lemon, sliced
A handful of rosemary
A handful of dried lavender
Petals from 1 tulip or 5 drops rose essential oil

SUMMER SIMMER POT

I love putting this on in the summer when my home needs a good cleanse. It's fresh, uplifting, and comforting all at once.

2 lemons, sliced
A handful of dried lavender
A handful of fresh mint
2 tablespoons vanilla extract

Psst *You can mix up the aromatics in glass jars and keep them, sealed, in your fridge if you don't want to simmer them right away or if you'd like to gift them!*

Styling an Open Kitchen Shelf

I *love* open shelving in a kitchen because it forces you to keep only what you need (raise your hand if, like me, you have a habit of buying beautiful ceramic mugs and dishes), and it doesn't hurt that a well-styled shelf looks beautiful, too. But how do you keep it functional while also stylish? Here are my tried-and-true tips!

Keep the essentials handy: Only display the dishware you frequently use. The items on this shelf are ones I use almost daily, so I don't have to worry about dust.

Make a display of books: If you don't have room for a cookbook wall, stack them on top of each other in groups and place items on top of the books to conserve space.

Create layers with art: To create layers and make your kitchen shelves more full, add framed prints behind your dishware. Secure the art to your backsplash or wall with a double-sided adhesive strip so it doesn't fall.

Everything counts: Even bottles of olive oil can be stylish! Buy oil in decorative jars and when they're empty, refill them.

If you don't have open shelving in your kitchen but love the look of it, a simple hack is to take the door off your existing kitchen cabinet. If there are holes down the side of the cabinet (to allow you to adjust the shelving placement), you can patch them with spackle or purchase plugs made to cover the holes at the hardware store. Remember, if you rent, store the extra door in a closet or under your bed so you can snap it back in place when you leave!

Kristy's Kitchen

This makeover was much more involved than Megan's, but if you are a homeowner like Kristy, you'll find some good tips here. Although Kristy had a bit more budget than the average renter (and no landlord), she didn't want to spend a ton of money to rip out cabinets and gut the entire kitchen, so she enlisted me to help.

BEFORE

A. Ripping out backsplash tile is time-consuming and expensive. It's a project that makes sense to tackle if you're ripping out countertops and appliances. If you aren't, opt for peel-and-stick tiles like these.

B. Get decorative with your cabinet handles. A mixture of oversized pulls and knobs creates a dynamic look.

C. If your fridge doesn't match the rest of your kitchen's style, cover it in peel-and-stick wallpaper.

D. To make your small kitchen feel more open, take off one of your cabinet doors and fill it with cookbooks and colorful dishware for an open-shelf look.

E. Line glass jars filled with dried goods along your countertop for easy access and a pop of color.

F. If your countertops are the worse for wear, go for peel-and-stick contact paper that looks like marble (but is actually laminate) for an elevated look.

G. If your ceilings are too low for a pendant light, opt for a stylish flush mount instead.

H. A new faucet will instantly make your kitchen feel brand new and is a quick and easy switch.

HOW TO | Paint Cabinets the Right Way

It took me numerous tries to nail cabinet painting, but I learned many lessons in the process. The most important thing I've learned about painting kitchen cabinets is that the transformation is *always* worth the effort . . . but there is definitely effort involved. You want to make sure you have enough space to lay your cabinets out to paint, and a space for them to dry. The process gets messy quickly, so ensuring you have a great setup is key! There are also different processes and materials needed depending on what is currently on your cabinets, as outlined below.

LAMINATE, VENEER, MDF, AND SOLID-WOOD CABINETS SEALED WITH A TOPCOAT

If your cabinets have a glossy finish, they are likely one of the materials listed above.

WHAT YOU'LL NEED

Screwdriver

Degreaser

Medium-grit sandpaper (anything between 120–220 grit) or electric sander

Lint-free cloth

High-adhesion, shellac-based primer

Two foam rollers or one paint sprayer

Paint (oil-based paint in a semigloss or a high-gloss finish)

INSTRUCTIONS

1. Remove the doors from the cabinets. Once removed, unscrew the knobs or pulls and cabinet hinges with a screwdriver.

2. Clean the surface of your cabinet doors with a degreaser so that the paint can stick to the surface. Sanding alone won't always take off grease.

3. Take gloss off with a medium-grit sandpaper (or an electric sander if you have one) and clean thoroughly with a lint-free cloth.

4. Apply two coats of a high-adhesion primer with a paint sprayer or foam roller to ensure that it sticks to your cabinet door. Let it dry completely before moving to the next step.

5. Apply the paint using a paint sprayer. A paint sprayer will always leave you with a smoother finish. You can rent these from most hardware stores or invest in a beginner one for under $100. I would *not* recommend spraying your cabinet doors inside. If you haven't meticulously covered your entire space with drop cloths, you'll risk finding a fine mist of paint covering surfaces that aren't meant to be painted. If you don't have access to a paint sprayer, use a small foam roller instead. They don't shed and will leave a smooth finish. Use an angled brush to get into the corners of your cabinets.

6. Lay your cabinet doors on an elevated surface and leave them to cure for a full 24 hours. The longer they have time to dry, the better, so the paint can harden and become more durable. Once they're dry, put the hinges back on and reattach the doors.

Psst — Try to keep your cabinets away from dust when they're drying so that it doesn't get caught in the paint.

UNTREATED OR PAINTED WOOD CABINETS

These cabinets won't have a glossy coat on top. They are less common but are easier to work with.

1

3

4

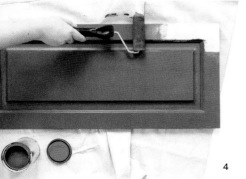

4

Screwdriver

Medium-grit sandpaper or electric sander

Lint-free cloth

Two foam rollers or paint sprayer

Water-based primer

Paint (latex-based paint in a semigloss, high-gloss, or satin finish)

INSTRUCTIONS

1. Remove the doors from the cabinets. Once removed, unscrew the knobs or pulls and cabinet hinges with a screwdriver.

2. Sand any paint off with medium-grit sandpaper or an electric sander until the surface is smooth. Clean thoroughly with a lint-free cloth.

3. Prime cabinets and let dry.

4. Once primer is dry, paint with a paint sprayer. A paint sprayer will always leave you with a smoother finish. You can rent these from most hardware stores or invest in a beginner one for under $100. I would *not* recommend spraying your cabinet doors inside. If you haven't meticulously covered your entire space with drop cloths, you'll risk finding a fine mist of paint covering surfaces that aren't meant to be painted. If you don't have access to a paint sprayer, use a small foam roller instead. They don't shed and will leave a smooth finish. Use an angled brush to get into the corners of your cabinets.

5. Lay your cabinet doors on an elevated surface and leave them to dry completely. The longer they have time to dry, the better so the paint can harden and become more durable. Once they're dry, put the hinges back on and reattach the doors.

Kitchen Supply Checklist

When I moved into my first apartment, I went to make something for dinner and realized I didn't have *anything* to cook with. I enlisted my mom to help me shop for kitchen supplies the next day, and I thought it would be helpful to have a list of kitchen essentials in one place that you can reference. I was so excited about making sure I loved everything I purchased, even if it was going into a drawer. Since that first apartment, I've tried to maintain that— you'll be surprised at how much joy beautiful salad servers can bring. Also, don't feel the need to purchase everything at once—just the basics to start will do!

- ❏ Can opener
- ❏ A couple of mixing bowls
- ❏ A set of good knives (You don't need to splurge on a block that comes stocked with every knife imaginable; just a bread knife, a small paring knife, and a larger chef's knife will do.)
- ❏ Measuring cups and spoons
- ❏ Vegetable peeler
- ❏ Spatula
- ❏ Colander
- ❏ Frying pan, large pot, and saucepan
- ❏ Cutting board
- ❏ A set of dishware:
  - ❏ dinner plates
  - ❏ pasta bowls
  - ❏ breakfast bowls
  - ❏ salad plates
  - ❏ small dipping bowls (I always seem to need more of these in my kitchen. They're great for entertaining and also for food prep.)

- ❏ A set of good glassware (My mistake is never buying glasses that are big enough! So opt for bigger rather than smaller.)
- ❏ Wooden spoons (four will do!)
- ❏ Big metal spoon
- ❏ Whisk
- ❏ Salad servers
- ❏ Tongs
- ❏ Baking sheet
- ❏ Glass or ceramic casserole dish

OPTIONAL (depending on how fancy you are in the kitchen!)

- ❏ Salad spinner
- ❏ Scale
- ❏ Potato masher

Snap and bring with you to shop!

Organizing a Pantry

If you're lucky enough to have a pantry, or even if you just have an extra cabinet dedicated to storing food, here are some ways to make whatever you have super cute and functional. This pantry was just an empty closet before I made it over with metal, portable shelving. To me, shelving that sits on the floor doesn't make use of vertical wall space, which means tons of wasted space. Instead, try a track shelving system that allows you to customize the height of each shelf, depending on what you are storing. It also means you are maximizing wall space.

A. Adorn the back of your closet or cabinet with wallpaper or wall decals for a fun pop of color and pattern.

B. Take all of your dried goods out of their packaging and organize them into glass jars with annotated labels. This will free up *tons* of space in your pantry or food cabinet and will look really great, too. Do the same things with spices. Cut the expiration date from the package and tape it to the bottom of the jar. If the food doesn't all fit in the jar, keep the overflow in a designated plastic bin that can be tucked away in your cabinet.

C. You can purchase really beautiful, stylized labels from small designers on Etsy. There's everything from modern style to farmhouse style labels to suit the rest of your kitchen.

D. Use floor baskets or bins to organize plastic bags.

E. Use trays to keep smaller items such as spices, oils, or other condiments corralled.

The Bedroom

I LOVE MAKING OVER

bedrooms. Unlike other rooms in your home, like kitchens and entryways that have to work extra hard functionally, the bedroom gives you much more of an opportunity to inject personality and really focus on the decor. When I was growing up, my bedroom was a place that I had free rein to decorate, and I would change it up continuously. I can remember just about every transformation it went through—a floating shelf in the corner for my keyboard that I asked my dad to install when I was seven; the purple gauze curtains I hung when I moved back home after a year in residence at university; my first queen-size bed that I adorned with a floral duvet and a mosquito net to keep it feeling extra whimsical. The constant in all my bedroom iterations was that each one felt like a safe place to land. I continue to view bedrooms this way—quiet, calm spaces that should provide us with a reprieve from the rest of the world. There's such an opportunity to have fun with texture to add warmth, and the bedroom is a space you can change often and easily with a switch in bedding and throw cushions. In this section, I'll outline the simplest ways to make your bedroom feel just like that.

Rayna's Bedroom

Rayna's "before" photos of this bedroom show the perfect example of a space that is oozing function but missing those few finishing touches that bring the warmth you should be looking for in a bedroom.

BEFORE

A. Paint the wall behind your bed a moody color to add depth and warmth. Try going for a softer color that's soothing.

B. Use a tray to corral nighttime accessories and stay organized.

C. To save money, purchase a downloadable piece of art and have it printed on canvas so it looks like a painting. You'll want it blown up to fill most of the wall above your bed—anything too small will make the room look and feel incomplete.

D. If you don't have room for table lamps, make use of your walls and hang a sconce.

E. Bring extra texture in through little details, like decorative curtain tiebacks.

F. Switch out boring knobs for something more ornate to make your nightstand or dresser look custom made.

G. Paint closet doors a fun color to add a decorative pop.

H. Adorn doorknobs with strings of pom-poms to add texture.

Who knew there was such a thing as cute tissue boxes?

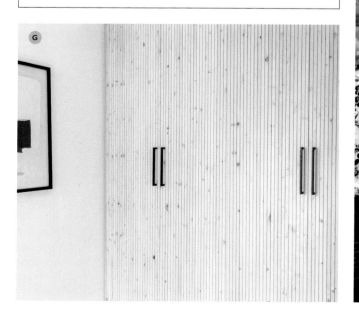

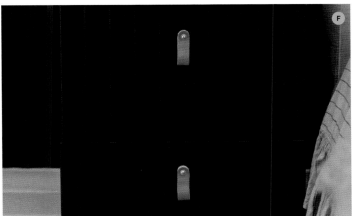

HOW TO | Make Your Bed Look Like It Belongs in a Hotel

Cozy doesn't have to mean fancy. Sometimes it's the simplest thing, like making your bed every morning, that will make your space feel warm and inviting. *But* if you've ever walked into a hotel and wondered how their beds always look so luxurious, here's how.

WHAT YOU'LL NEED

Fitted sheet

Top sheet

Two comforters

Two Euro shams

Two sleeping pillows

A decorative lumbar pillow

Quilt

INSTRUCTIONS

1. Don't use exactly matching fitted and top sheets. I love using the same color in two different shades (for example, a light pink color for the fitted sheet and a darker, richer pink for the top sheet). Place the top sheet with the pattern side down so that the decorative side shows when you fold it over the duvet.

2. The trick to making your bed extra fluffy is placing one extra comforter, folded into thirds, in the center or at the end of your bed, on top of the first duvet. This comforter can be either neutral (but textured) or patterned (if your main duvet cover is a solid color).

3. Now time for pillows! My favorite combination for beds is two 26 by 26 inch (66 by 66 cm) solid Euro shams that rest against the headboard, two sleeping pillows with cases that match the color of the fitted sheet, and one decorative lumbar pillow in front. The number and size of pillows depends on the size of your frame. For a king-size bed, you want to use three Euro shams and ensure that your sleeping pillows are also king size. You might find a longer lumbar pillow better fills the bed.

4. Place a quilt on top of the second comforter. You can mix and match colors and patterns, but to keep everything looking cohesive, stick within similar color tones.

HOW TO

DIY Custom Wardrobe Fronts

In Rayna's bedroom, she had dressers lining the back wall for her clothes. While dressers are a bedroom go-to, I find that in smaller spaces they waste valuable vertical wall space. I got rid of the dressers and instead filled the wall with floor-to-ceiling wardrobes, which gave her much more storage. I wanted to make them look a little fancier, so I wrapped them in pine that was custom cut into strips to get a fluted look.

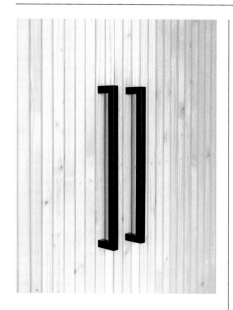

WHAT YOU'LL NEED

Measuring tape

Pine panels (or any other wood you like the look of!)

Table saw

Wood glue

Shim in the width you want the gap between strips to be

Nail gun

Wood filler

150 grit sandpaper or electric sander

Clear shellac

Paintbrush

Decorative handles

Drill

INSTRUCTIONS

1. Measure the height of your wardrobe.

2. With your table saw, cut enough 1 inch (2.5 cm) strips of pine to cover the front and sides of your wardrobe.

3. Adhere each piece of pine to the cabinet with wood glue. Place a shim between each piece to ensure the distance between each strip is equal.

4. Use a nail gun along each strip to secure it. Make sure the holes from the nails are in the same spot on each piece, so the holes look uniform overall.

5. Cover each nail with wood filler.

6. Sand down the pine and paint a clear shellac on top with a paintbrush to make it glossy and durable.

7. Add large, decorative handles with a drill.

Bedroom Organization

In almost *every* bedroom or studio apartment makeover I tackle, I add under-bed storage. Under the bed is the most underused space for storage, and there are so many storage options that you can add, including drawers with wheels or decorative baskets with lids. Store everything from seasonal items to free up your entryway space to extra linens if you don't have closet space. Make sure to measure the space under your bed before you buy organizers!

One thing I learned when I had one tiny closet in my bedroom in The Treehouse was that bedroom closets see no bounds when it comes to the kinds of things that can be organized in them. In my tiny closet I stored not only my clothing but also my luggage, overflow toiletry items, and anything else I could neatly tuck away. Though you can't add closet space, you *can* maximize space, and here's how:

A. Add a fun pop of color and pattern by using peel-and-stick wallpaper to decorate the back of your closet.

B. If you share a closet with someone else, designate a side for each person. Use different-colored clothing hangers for each person.

C. Make use of the space below the clothing with a dresser or laundry hamper.

D. Maximize vertical space all the way to the top of the closet by stacking baskets. Store sweaters, bathing suits, and extra linens up high, and make sure to label the baskets with gift tags so you know what's in them.

E. Don't forget about the doors! There are tons of over-the-door organizers for things like shoes or handbags. These organizers are great for holding smaller items like sunglasses.

F. Pack smaller luggage inside large suitcases.

G. Use an open clothing rack to display your favorite pieces.

H. Invest in a bed with storage drawers underneath.

Ways to Pack Organization into Your Bedroom

Maximizing your space is important, but don't forget to keep things tidy, too! These tips will help you to keep your extra bedroom space just as neat and organized as the rest of your home.

Have a bar cart double as a nightstand.

Put a dresser in your closet to make use of empty space underneath your clothing.

Make use of the back of your bedroom door with over-the-door hooks. They're renter friendly and a great place to store bags and other accessories.

If you have room for a bench at the end of your bed, try to find one that has storage, and make it work double-duty to hold linens or other items.

Lindsay's Bedroom

When Lindsay purchased her home, her bedroom came as a standard, cookie-cutter box without a lot of personality. She wanted to keep the room airy, neutral, and bright but still warm, with subtle hits of color. There are a few ways you can make a bright, white room still feel cozy.

BEFORE

A. Opt for a creamy white with yellow undertones—it'll make the space feel warmer.

B. Get decorative with your curtain rods to add texture, which will in turn make your space feel cozier.

C. Frame a piece of wallpaper or gift wrap to save on the cost of art.

D. Float books on the wall for a functional and stylish display.

E. Keep the larger pieces in your bedroom neutral and add color through accessories that you can easily change, like cushions and rugs.

F. Add personality to white furniture by switching out knobs to something textured.

G. White walls can be interesting! Install decorative molding with a nail gun and paint it the same color as your wall. There are also peel-and-stick wall molding kits if you're a renter!

The Treehouse Bedroom

I loved the bedroom in my first apartment. Because it was on the third floor, it really felt like a cozy loft space. I utilized all of the angled walls with built-in shelves for extra storage, and my bed fit perfectly under the slanted roof. When I moved in, one of the walls was painted a dark navy blue, and the previous tenant's furniture was dark, even the curtains. My goal was to completely brighten up the space, and it's amazing how much bigger it felt, even with a king-size bed, with just a few tweaks.

A. If you're battling with a dark space, opt for white curtains. These are black-out curtains, so they block the light.

B. If you don't have room for nightstands, use the top of a dresser or floating shelves on the wall instead.

C. Embrace low ceilings with a big pendant light, as long as it isn't placed where people walk—this one hovered over the end of the bed.

D. A shelf like this doesn't have to just hold books. Use it to store shoes or clothing concealed in baskets.

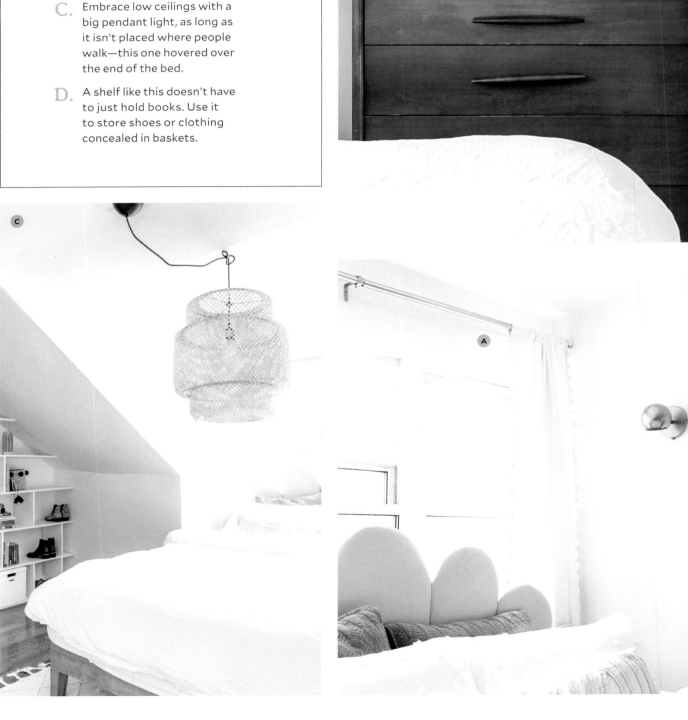

HOW TO

Make Plug-in Wall Sconces Look Hardwired

There was no space in my bedroom for night tables (even if I had a smaller bed!), but I needed some reading light. There was no place to hardwire sconces, and I didn't want plug-in cords out in the open, so I decided to make my own battery-powered sconces that looked hardwired.

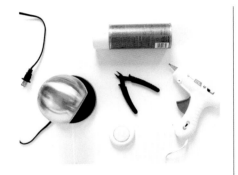

WHAT YOU'LL NEED

Wire cutters

Wired wall sconce

Primer

Multi-purpose spray paint that sticks to metal

Paper

Tape

Glue gun

Puck light with remote control

Drill

INSTRUCTIONS

1. Using wire cutters, cut the cord from the wall sconce.

2. Spray the whole light with primer and then paint. Stuff the inside with paper and tape it in place so the spray paint doesn't get inside.

3. Using a glue gun, affix the puck light to the lightbulb socket. Buy a puck light with a battery port that's accessible by taking the top off or you won't be able to change the batteries once it's been glued!

4. Hang the sconce on the wall with a drill and the hardware provided. Use the puck light's remote to turn it on and off.

1

2

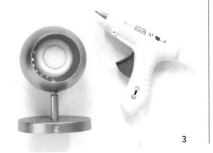

3

Renter Friendly!

The
Living
Room

GROWING UP, WE HAD A

denim sofa in our living room. It was cushy and sank in when you sat down, enveloping your entire body in a safe cocoon. It sat in front of the large window that faced our street and over the years the sun bleached the denim so the back of it looked almost white. And while this sofa was a spectacle for anyone who visited (my friends had never seen anything like it), what I remember most about it was how comfy it was. In many ways, that sofa held me through a lot of big life changes: It's where I sat when we brought our first cat, Harriet, home when she was eight weeks old; it's where I found out I was accepted to university; and it's where I experienced heartbreaks, goodbyes, and celebrations.

Not every piece of furniture you own should and will hold all of the sentimental weight of the world, but I do think that the items we choose to place in our homes should hold us, like that denim sofa did for me, through the highs and lows of life. I truly believe that feeling comfortable and good in your space can make those tough times a little easier to bear.

In this next section, I show you how to make your living room feel like yours—how to take a secondhand sofa and make it custom and what to do with that awkward nook in the corner that's never been filled.

Jenn's Living Room

J enn's living room is bigger than a lot of rental apartment living rooms I've seen but all the furniture was pushed up against the walls, causing the room to look like one big space with no obvious layout and flow. The goal of this makeover was to create a space where Jenn could lounge and host. Floating some furniture in the middle of the room created a more unified, cozy space that's perfect for entertaining.

BEFORE

Kafka The Complete Stories
METAMORPHOSIS AND OTHER STORIES

A. Because there was no television to center the sofa to, I instead created a conversation area with two lounge chairs, which help fills the open room. You can re-create this layout if your television is mounted on the wall, but I find it works best in rooms without a TV.

B. There is such a thing as stylish ceiling fans if your space needs one!

C. Place a mirror in the sightline of an art print for a stylish reflection. Mirrors bring natural light into a dark space because they bounce the light.

D. I searched for a paint color in a slightly darker green than the sofa cover for the walls to create a monochromatic color scheme. Don't worry if the colors aren't exactly the same, as long as they are similar tones.

E. Awkward nooks are always a great place for a bar cart.

F. Upcycle a boring cabinet with a custom wood top and custom legs. This one is from a piece of countertop from a kitchen island.

G. Album covers make great wall art. Attach holders with heavy-duty double-sided tape that adheres to brick.

H. Arched floor lamps make a great lighting source for larger living rooms because they fill horizontal and vertical space that would otherwise go unused.

I. In a large, open area, remember to use a rug that fills the room. A rug that is too small will veto any flow and make the living space feel tinier than it is.

J. Pet beds can be cute, too!

K. This thrifted sofa used to be gray and lacked personality. Learn how I transformed it into a mid-century modern dream on page 198.

HOW TO | Hack Your Ikea Sofa

So you really want a pink-velvet sofa (which is completely understandable), but you're not up for spending thousands on it, especially when you know it could become dated in a few years. I hear you. Which is why I'm going to share one of my *favorite* ways to upcycle an Ikea sofa that will give you the flexibility to bring trendy colors and materials into your home whenever you feel like it. This hack was a lifesaver for my partner and me when we moved in together, because it meant we could compromise by switching it up between both a pink *and* hunter-green sofa throughout the year and appease both our styles. There are tons of Ikea sofa models on Facebook Marketplace or Kijiji, making this a budget-friendly and sustainable way to upgrade a tired piece of furniture.

Renter Friendly!

WHAT YOU'LL NEED

An Ikea sofa (even an old sofa model that Ikea no longer carries will work!)

Sofa cover (from a company that sells slipcovers made especially for Ikea furniture)

Fancy new legs (from a company that sells legs made especially for Ikea furniture)

A drill (if necessary)

INSTRUCTIONS

1. Purchase a slipcover for the model of your sofa. If you're unsure what model of sofa you have, it will likely say on the tag of the old slipcover.

2. Remove the old slipcover and replace it with your fancy new one.

3. Flip the sofa over and unscrew the legs. Screw in your new ones. If the company sends you a new bracket that needs to be installed with the legs, screw it in using a drill.

Where to Buy Slipcovers

These companies sell custom slipcovers in just about every fabric—linen, velvet, and cotton—that are custom made to fit just about any model, old or new, of Ikea sofas. Most of them also sell slipcovers for Ikea armchairs and ottomans. Many—if not all—Ikea sofas have removable slipcovers, making them easily interchangeable. Many of these companies also sell legs for Ikea cabinets and sofas.

Bemz: This is where my velvet sofa slipcovers are from. Bemz will also send you free fabric samples. You can choose from a regular fit or loose fit, which gives a more casual look.

Comfort Works: This company makes slipcovers that fit sofas from popular decor stores, including Ikea, West Elm, and Restoration Hardware.

Prettypegs: This company's unique furniture legs add tons of personality to Ikea storage units, beds, tables, and sofas. They come in almost every color, design, style, and height to transform your sofa into just about any style—from mid-century modern hairpin legs to low-to-the-ground minimalistic ones made from wood.

Rayna's Living Room

The biggest challenge in Rayna's living space was sofa placement, which I know is common when you're trying to fit furniture into a small space. If the sofa were to face the fireplace and in turn the television (which couldn't be placed anywhere else because of outlet location), it would really close off the room, and there'd be no space for any other seating or a coffee table. If you're working with a similar layout to this, where the sofa isn't able to face the television, you can still make your lounge area feel intimate and functional.

BEFORE

A. If your space can't fit a standard-size coffee table, opt for two small side tables side-by-side to keep the flow of the space moving. You can easily move them around when you have guests over.

B. Frame a fireplace with floating shelves to hold decorative items and add more storage.

C. Hide the router with an art print.

D. No pendant light? Make use of floor lights or battery-powered sconces like this one.

E. Keep a space cozy by placing seating across the room to create a conversation area.

F. Curtains will always add softness.

G. Store coffee-table books in a non-working fireplace for stylish storage.

H. There are lots of YouTube channels that will make your television look like a piece of art.

Calyssa's Living Room

I loved taking on Calyssa's living room makeover because she was looking for a Scandi-style space that was quite neutral but still cozy. Sometimes when we're working with lots of neutral colors like creams and whites, it can be a challenge to keep the space from feeling sterile and cold. But it's easier than it looks, especially if you follow these simple steps:

BEFORE

A. Varying tones of whites, creams, and grays are key to keeping a neutral space from feeling cold (see page 70 for neutral color palette ideas).

B. You can still have an accent wall in a neutral space, but keep it within a similar soft color family.

C. An awkward nook is a great spot for a dining area. A tall bar table will save space.

D. Yes, there is such a thing as fashionable pendant cords! Opt for a macrame one so it looks stylish out in the open.

E. Textured accessories and furniture are key to keeping a neutral space feel cozy—try velvet fabrics, woven baskets, wicker, jute, and linen curtains.

F. When styling a shelf, layer in personal trinkets and turn items into art by putting them on display.

G. Hits of black accents will ground your neutral space and add balance.

The Bathroom

GROWING UP, WHEN WE WOULD STAY AT MY AUNT
Samantha's home in England, I loved using her bathroom. Weird, I know, but hear me out: The bathroom used to be a bedroom, so the old wood floor that spanned the rest of the bedrooms was carried into the bathroom, and a working fireplace greeted you on the opposite wall when you walked in. The room was huge, with a tub against the back wall, a shower next to it, and walls that held a huge piece of art on canvas in a bold blue and red color palette. There was a cozy Persian rug in the middle of the room and an old wooden wall cabinet that held little amber bottles of essential oils. I remember always thinking that this room didn't *feel* like a bathroom but instead a real, cozy *room*. Although I know this kind of bathroom is an anomaly for most, the idea of it being a space that felt like a room rather than just a cold, tucked-away box has always stuck with me and I'm always struck by how many people *don't* view these spaces in this way. In many of the spaces I visit to scout or make over, the bathroom is the room that's left behind, the door kept closed so no one sees what's behind it unless absolutely necessary. It makes sense to me: Bathrooms covered in outdated tile seem like an impossible feat to transform, not to mention pricey. And although there are ways to cover outdated tile with peel-and-stick products or tile paint (both of which I cover in this section), if there's one thing to take away from this section it's that bathrooms should be treated as if they're part of the rest of your home, instead of tucked away for no one to see.

Whether you take the plunge and cover your outdated floor in peel-and-stick vinyl or instead just add simple decor touches like a new shower curtain and a cute piece of wall art, the goal of the next section is to help you approach the way you see this room—one that deserves to feel cozy and warm just like the rest of your home—and in turn the way you feel in this room, too.

The Treehouse Bathroom

When I moved into my first apartment, I had a clear vision for every room except this bathroom. There was no closed storage, the walls were painted yellow, the flooring looked like it belonged in a gym changing room, and it was dark. Turns out this was the room that pushed me the most creatively, and I was able to try so many fun renter-friendly solutions that took this bathroom from blah to super cute.

BEFORE

A. This floor treatment is completely reversible! See page 214 to learn how.

B. Switch out rental sconces and go bold with something decorative—it will shine (literally and figuratively) in the small space.

C. If you have no cabinet space, place toilet paper in a decorative basket.

D. Find clever ways to hang a slim storage cabinet, like narrow indents or gaps in the wall so it doesn't take up too much space.

E. Little decorative dishes and small bowls are a great way to organize small items like hair ties, cotton face pads, and soap.

F. A floating shelf above your sink can hold daily necessities—just make sure they're in decorative containers.

G. Buy amber apothecary-style bottles and fill them with soap.

H. Make use of empty space above a cabinet with stackable containers for even more storage.

I. Opt for a hanging plant instead of a shade to keep your small space feeling bright (that is, if your window doesn't face a street!)

J. Keep overflow toiletries in your bedroom closet, neatly organized in a basket.

HOW TO | Install Peel-and-Stick Flooring

Believe it or not, you can buy vinyl peel-and-stick flooring to cover outdated floor tile. It can be purchased in either vinyl squares—which is great to cover up large ceramic bathroom tiles—or vinyl panels very similar to the backsplash mentioned on page 149 (and what I used in The Treehouse bathroom). Peel-and-stick flooring is completely waterproof and can be used over most smooth surfaces like ceramic tiles, sealed concrete, or linoleum. The best part is that it is completely renter friendly and removed the same way as backsplash tiles, with a hit of heat from a hairdryer. Unlike a lot of other flooring, peel-and-stick flooring is super easy to install with no power tools, grout, or adhesive needed. These products are installed the same way as peel-and-stick wallpaper (see page 94). For those tricky areas around the toilet or sink, follow these steps for a smooth install.

Psst *Consider tile paint for the shower area instead of peel-and-stick tile because it is waterproof and mold resistant.*

Snap and bring with you to shop!

WHAT YOU'LL NEED

A putty knife or a small card (anything with a flat edge will do!)

Utility knife

Caulk

INSTRUCTIONS

1. Carry the sheet of vinyl up the base of your toilet and sink.

2. Using a putty knife or small card, crease the vinyl around the curves.

3. Use your utility knife to cut away the vinyl.

4. Once the tile is stuck to the floor and trimmed, caulk around the base of the toilet and sink to hide any imperfections.

My Favorite Places to Shop for Peel-and-Stick Flooring

FloorPops: This company's durable flooring comes in squares and is available in hundreds of colors and patterns.

Quadrostyle: This is where I purchased peel-and-stick flooring in sheets, similar to wallpaper, for The Treehouse flooring.

Etsy: This great marketplace is perfect for discovering peel-and-stick flooring.

Psst *A contour gauge tool is a useful way to trace the shape of the toilet or cabinet onto vinyl flooring so you get a perfect cut.*

Janelle's and Christine's Powder Rooms

Despite powder rooms (defined as any bathroom without a shower) being small, there's such an opportunity to go bold with your decor, especially because they're not the main bathroom in a home. I always love a patterned wallpaper in any room, but there's something so much more impactful about walking into a small space that's been covered in an adventurous print. Because powder rooms are so small, I often recommend the same basic tips for anyone, which can be found on the next two pages.

BEFORE

A. Replace outlet covers to match the color of the wallpaper, or cover them with the wallpaper, too.

B. A little open shelf is perfect to hold hand cream or extra soap for your guests. Bonus points if it's also a towel holder!

C. If there's no closed storage, place toilet paper in a decorative basket on top of the toilet.

D. Thrifted artwork in mismatched frames is a budget-friendly way to decorate a wall.

E. Layer in other thrifted pieces to break up all the frames.

F. Let your wallpaper dictate the style of fixtures you choose. This wavy mirror complements the organic shapes in the wallpaper.

G. You can also use peel-and-stick backsplash tiles in bathrooms!

H. If there's no counter space, make use of wall space by attaching a soap dispenser to the wall.

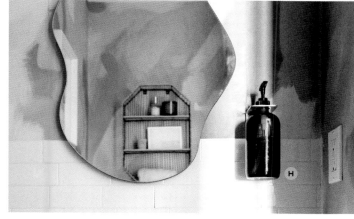

Alexandra's Bathroom

When I moved into my current home, this bathroom was a dream because of its size, and I wanted to make it feel like a cozy extension of the rest of the rooms in our home. I love this bathroom, and decorating this space taught me how to lean into fixtures in a space that might not be my first choice. Unlike The Treehouse bathroom, I knew I couldn't cover the tile with peel-and-stick products because there was so much of it. But to be honest, I started to embrace it as I began adding my own decorative elements. If you move into a home where the bathroom is *covered* in tile, there are ways to add your own touch to it while also embracing the existing decor.

BEFORE

A. Embrace the tile color palette by weaving colors through your accessories. This black-and-white shower curtain complements both my style and the original fixtures.

B. Switching out a faucet is easy and will instantly elevate your bathroom.

C. Runners aren't just for hallways, and will make your bathroom feel cozy and warm. Pair them with a bathmat, of course, for practicality. You can also buy bathmats that look like decorative runners.

D. If you have a potted plant with long stems, like a pothos, gently attach the trailing vines to the wall with damage-free, removable hooks.

E. A large basket for towels or laundry adds texture.

F. Don't forget about art! Just make sure it's in a frame that's tightly sealed so your art doesn't warp in the humid environment.

G. Replace your cabinet legs with something custom to bring personality to boring storage.

The Entryway

AH, THE ENTRYWAY. MOSTLY A DISTANT DREAM WHEN
you live in a small space, am I right? In my first apartment, there was a tiny landing at the top of the stairs leading to my apartment. When you walked through my apartment door, it led straight into the living room, which left absolutely no space for clutter caused by jackets or shoes. I had to get crafty and find closed-storage solutions, which are essential in a small-space entryway. I think for many people, the design of an entryway is solely practical. And while that is absolutely true, there is something to be said for how this is the first space anyone sees (including you!) when walking through the front door. Whether you're creating comfort by placing a battery-powered table lamp on the entryway credenza or setting down a doormat with a cute welcome graphic, I'm here to assure you that this space can be one you love, no matter how awkward or nonexistent your entryway is.

Rayna's Entryway

Rayna's entryway merges into her living room space, without any clear divide between the two, which is such a common layout if you live in a small space. Although it's fairly roomy, the furniture in the "before" wasn't working double-duty, causing the space to feel underutilized. When you sit down to design your entryway, always think about the function of the space first, before the decor, and ask yourself how you need it to work for you.

BEFORE

A. These shelving units were in the living room but function much better in the entryway.

B. I put a bench between them to create a seating area with a custom cushion top.

C. Baskets are the secret to ensuring everything you need to store in this space has a home. Create piles of what you need to store before you buy baskets so you know what sizes you need.

D. Wall hooks are functional, but can also be a statement. Hang them at different heights for a fun look.

E. Create separation with paint that's a different color than your living room.

F. This shoe cabinet has a slim profile but stores so many shoes. Customize it with a wood top and new knobs.

G. Painting the shoe cabinet the same color as the wall gives it a built-in look.

H. A cozy runner will warm up your entryway. Bonus points if it can be washed!

I. Don't forget a mirror! It will make your space feel bigger and you'll be able to take a glance at yourself before you head out.

Amanda's Entryway

This was a standard cookie-cutter condo entryway before I made it over. And sometimes, a truly blank slate like this one can be overwhelming, but don't worry. Depending on your style, adding some color into a small area like this can set the tone for the rest of your home and make a boring space feel welcoming.

BEFORE

A. Peel-and-stick wallpaper in an interesting pattern adds personality.

B. This art piece is covering a circuit box. You always want to have easy access to your circuit box, so don't hang anything too heavy!

C. A tiny stool with a removable top is great for putting on shoes and adding extra storage.

D. This light isn't hardwired! See page 190 on how to DIY your own.

E. If you have high ceilings, draw your eye up and fill a blank wall with a large art piece.

F. Use visually interesting knobs as wall hooks! Hang them at different heights to add a decorative moment.

G. Opt for a vinyl mat if a standard doormat won't fit under your door. This one looks like tile, is waterproof, and is easy to clean.

Psst Only store what's needed in your entryway to keep clutter at bay. Store seasonal items in bins under your bed or on the top shelf of your closet.

The Treehouse Entryway

Outside my apartment door, I had a little landing at the top of the stairs that led to my unit. Squished onto that tiny landing was shoe storage and an over-the-door hook for jackets. Inside, this cabinet (which actually held my cat's litter box! See page 236 for the DIY) was the perfect credenza for keys and mail. Having essentially no entryway taught me how to maximize a small space while also keeping it clutter-free. Here are my favorite organizing essentials for a teeny-tiny entryway that are also renter friendly:

A dresser: If you have the space, thrift an old dresser and fill it with hats, scarves, helmets, sports gear, and more. The top can be used for mail and keys.

Baskets: If you have any shelving in your entryway, maximize any and all vertical space with baskets. If you have room for more than one, stack them. Floor baskets also work well for anything that's grab-and-go, like winter hats and mitts.

A coat rack: If you don't have any closet space and can't hang hooks on the wall, use a coat rack. Just ensure it's good quality—if you get an inexpensive one, it won't last.

Key dish: Never misplace your keys again by placing a small dish near the front door.

A hall tree with bench: Invest in an entryway unit that maximizes vertical space with hooks and has a bench at the bottom for storage.

Living with Pets

MY FAMILY CAT, HARRIET, PASSED AWAY WHEN SHE

was seventeen. Mine since I was twelve, she had been my companion for over half my life. Less than a year before she passed away, Lottie (and before you ask, because I know you will: Yes, Lottie is a Ragdoll!) came into my life, and in a lot of ways she embodies home for me, as did Harriet. In short, I know how integral pets are to our daily home lives.

I get a *ton* of questions about how to decorate if you have pets—where you put a cat's litter box if you live in a small space, what fabrics to use and how to make everything they come with look, well, cute. I'll answer all those questions and more in this section.

HOW TO

Make a Hidden DIY Litter Box Cabinet

When I moved into The Treehouse, I tried putting my cat's litter box in so many places—tucked behind my bedroom door (wouldn't recommend falling asleep to the smell of cat litter), in the bathroom (there was absolutely no room for this, unless I wanted to step over it to use the toilet), tucked beside my sofa (guests *loved* that)—until I realized I needed to think a little more outside the box. Enter the hidden cat litter box cabinet, which can be DIY'd with just about any existing cabinet. When I tell you this was a game changer for my entire apartment, I'm not lying. It conceals the box, the smell, and those little bits of litter that used to end up throughout my entire home.

WHAT YOU'LL NEED

Cabinet of your choice (untreated wood is the easiest to customize)

Cat flap (including template and instructions for installation)

Pencil

Jigsaw (if your cabinet is made from wood)

Wire cutters (if your cabinet is made from metal)

Drill

Paint (if your cabinet is made from untreated wood, use a latex-based paint. If it's made from metal, use an oil-based paint. If it's an Ikea piece that has a glossy finish, see page 132 for how to paint Ikea furniture that has a laminate finish for precise steps.)

Cane webbing

Staple gun

Legs (if your cabinet doesn't have any already)

Decorative knobs

Renter Friendly!

INSTRUCTIONS

1. Determine which side of the cabinet the cat flap will be on.

2. Using the template that comes with the cat flap, trace an outline with a pencil. That will be the cat's "door."

3. Cut out the door with the jigsaw. Note: For a metal cabinet, use wire cutters to install the cat flap, not a jigsaw!

4. Paint your cabinet a fun color (see painting cabinets on page 162).

5. Install the cat flap by following the instructions that came with it. It will hide any jagged or imperfect edges that you made with your jigsaw! Note: If you aren't confident your cat will use the pet flap, create an open archway instead.

6. Using the jigsaw, cut out arches on the front doors of your cabinet and attach cane webbing using a staple gun.

7. The cane webbing will keep the air flowing inside the cabinet, so it doesn't become a smelly mess inside.

8. Add custom legs and knobs with a drill.

9. Put the litter box inside and remember to show your cat where their new washroom is! Treats may be necessary.

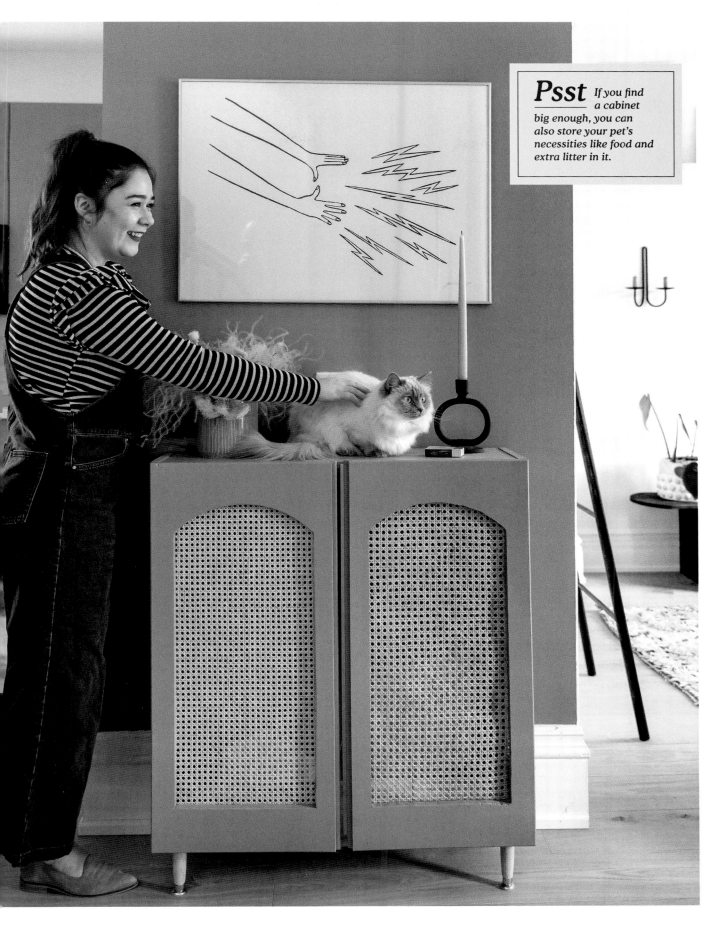

Psst *If you find a cabinet big enough, you can also store your pet's necessities like food and extra litter in it.*

Pet-Friendly Fabrics

I'll be honest, I never had to worry about Lottie or Harriet scratching the furniture, and I consider myself very lucky! I know that's not the case for everyone, so here's what I've learned when it comes to the best fabrics if you live with pets.

If you have a cat that scratches, velvet-covered furniture is a good option because it has a short pile. That means there are no little threads for your cat to pull out from the fabric. The downside is that velvet fabric does attract pet hair. I don't mind using a lint roller or vacuum cleaner to clean the hair off my velvet sofa, though.

Microfiber material is one of the best choices if you have pets because it's easy to clean and difficult for your pet to rip. The downside is that microfiber sofas aren't always the most stylish option—but they are practical.

Leather is also a great material because it is easy to clean and hair doesn't stick to it as easily as other fabrics. The downside is that it easily shows scratch marks; if you have a pet with sharp nails that likes to scratch, any imperfections will likely show.

Ways to Bring Style into Your Home with Pets

Although pets come with a lot of stuff, that doesn't mean your home has to be cluttered with dull pet furniture and accessories. In fact, there are *tons* of amazing pet products on the market for decor lovers that will only enhance the look of your home.

Media consoles and side tables: Some companies sell these pieces of furniture with built-in spots for pets, which is great for small spaces!

Ceramic pet bowls: There are lots of small makers that make stylish options. You could even use beautiful cereal bowls, too.

Decorative wood tray or colorful silicone mats: These can serve as pet bowl mats to keep your floors clean.

Pet beds that mimic trendy decor pieces: Woven rattan hanging cat swings, miniature sofas, and floor baskets are all fun options.

Cat scratchers: We often think of cat scratchers as being bulky and unsightly, but if you use "boho cat scratchers" as a search term, there are some stylish and sleek options.

Studio Apartments

SOME OF THE MOST POPULAR VIDEOS ON MY CHANNEL

are makeovers of studio apartments, and it's not lost on me that the video that started my whole career when I was at *Chatelaine* was a studio apartment makeover. In fact, my series *Studio Fix*, where I make over bachelor apartments under 500 square feet, has racked up over 11 million views and counting.

When shooting these videos, my team and I (which is about five of us on set) cram into these one-room abodes with tools, painting supplies, our makeover kit, all of the furniture in dozens of boxes, and our camera and lighting equipment. Somehow, we make it work and are able to transform these tiny rooms into functional and beautiful homes with multipurpose zones. Revealing these spaces to the makeover recipient is unlike any other space because it's not just one room—it's their entire home—and because of that, it feels more significant than usual.

When people ask me why I think *Studio Fix* is my most-watched series, I tell them I think it's because people finally relate to the spaces they see on my channel—I started my channel for those who live in tiny spaces, the ones that are often forgotten in shiny magazines or coffee-table books, and *Studio Fix* encapsulates that. The goal of this section is to combine all the information in that series in one place, so that you can feel empowered to make your tiny space feel like a home.

Margaree's Studio

As soon as I walked into Margaree's studio apartment, I knew it was special. Even though it's a small space, the apartment is filled with character—wood floors, a built-in hutch, and tons of light that pours through the windows. The biggest challenge is, unsurprisingly, size. Margaree works, lounges, entertains, and sleeps in this space, and because it's entirely open, things can look cluttered easily. How do you create a visual divide between areas in a tiny, open space? And is it even possible to have work/life balance when you are staring at your desk all day? I'll answer these questions and give you tips on studio apartment layouts similar to this one because yes, it is absolutely possible to have it all (and more!) even if you are working with 300 square feet or less.

BEFORE

A. Creating designated zones in a studio apartment will visually separate spaces within the open space.

B. A custom cane-webbing headboard designates this nook as the bedroom. All you need is a headboard frame, a staple gun, and some cane webbing to DIY this.

C. Two small lounge chairs facing the sofa enclose this area and create a defined living room space.

D. Make sure your rug spans the entire living room zone so that all the furniture sits on top of it to better define the area.

E. If you have any open space that isn't being put to use, a bench not only looks great but can be used as extra seating when guests come over.

F. Create any separation you can between your work and living space. This could be as simple as tucking your laptop under your sofa at the end of the day.

G. Large floor mirrors are incredibly expensive. This one was upcycled from a mirrored closet that was thrifted for under fifty dollars.

If you don't have anywhere for a television, use a projector screen that can roll up instead.

Scott's Studio

Before I made over Scott's studio, he had arranged his furniture perfectly, as if in a game of Tetris. Scott's apartment is *small*—less than 350 square feet—but he was adamant that he didn't want the size of his space to inhibit him from doing the things he loved, like entertaining and playing video games comfortably from his sofa. He also needed a work-from-home space and bike storage.

BEFORE

A. Though expensive, Murphy beds (which are beds installed in a cabinet on a wall) are an incredible solution if you have a small space that needs to function in many ways. This one also turns into a sofa when not in use.

B. Make use of vertical space by storing your bike on the wall. There are many bike racks like this one that also double as entryway shelves or have built-in storage cubbies.

C. Collapsible furniture is key. This arm expands when Scott is working to create an L-shaped desk.

D. This coffee table folds down and is stored easily when the bed is out.

E. Turn your everyday items into art! Function and style at its finest.

Other Ways to Create a Workspace in a Tiny Apartment

A small side table that slides over your sofa arm will create a portable workstation.

A ladder desk makes use of wall space and allows you to store work necessities or books in baskets up top.

A drop-leaf table can be a desk by day and dining table by night.

Wall cabinets that fold out into tables are perfect for saving floor space.

If your only option is working from the dining table, create a WFH utility cart that holds stationery, your laptop, chargers, and notebooks. At the end of the day, make sure it all goes back on the cart, and tuck it into a corner out of the way.

Creating
Closed Storage

"Storage" and "studio apartments" aren't words you often associate together. In all the studios I have made over, storage is always at the top of the list of challenges. It makes sense—you're already trying to fit about six rooms into one without any walls! Here are some tried-and-true storage solutions I turn to when tackling spaces for my *Studio Fix* series.

Capitalize on vertical wall space: When you're short on square footage, store upward with floating wall shelves.

Make use of the tops of cabinetry: If your bookshelf or cabinets don't go all the way to the ceiling, slide a storage bin on top filled with things you don't reach for often. A folding step ladder will help you access these bins and can be tucked away easily.

Create a visual divide: Place a free-floating shelf in the middle of the room to act as a divider and storage area.

Baskets, always: Use baskets to hide clutter and add decoration. Make sure they're sturdy!

Ditch the full-length dining table: Folding tables are your BFF. Install a Murphy-style table in your kitchen or living space and unfold it only when you need it.

The Cloffice

Hands down, my favorite makeover in The Treehouse was my cloffice, which may not be a word in the dictionary, but is well known in the design community. When I started my business, I didn't even have a dining table, so I knew I had to forgo very valuable closet real estate and turn mine into a tiny home office instead. It was the perfect nook for me to work from, and a few months later when I did have a dining table, the closet turned into a storage area for all of my files, tech, and camera gear. My cloffice remains one of my favorite projects because I really did prove to myself that if I have a need for more space and a vision, I can make it happen, even when there's no obvious solution. As my business began to grow bigger and work/life balance seemed sometimes out of control, the ability to close the door at the end of the day was a game changer. Even if you don't have a door you can close, sometimes setting those boundaries is as easy as tucking your laptop under your sofa at the end of the day, or using paint to visually separate your work area from your living area.

A. Paint or wallpaper the closet a fun color to differentiate it from the rest of the room.

B. Continue the color or wallpaper on the outside of the door and change the knob for a custom look.

C. A shelf above the desk can hold a printer and files.

D. A floating vanity doubles as a desk.

E. A pegboard is a great way to make use of wall space and organize stationery for easy access.

F. Use a floor basket to hold (and hide) tech clutter like cords and chargers.

G. Don't forget about lightning. Switching your light out for something decorative will make this feel more like a room than a closet!

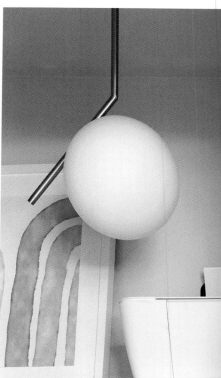

i just ate
a box of
wheat thins
for dinner
and another
friend got
engaged

DIY an Air Conditioner Cover/Side Table

When I was planning Austen's studio apartment makeover, I hate to admit that I almost gave up because of his air conditioner unit. Hear me out—it was taking up extremely valuable wall real estate. He nixed the idea of having a Murphy bed, and I couldn't figure out how I was going to create a functional space with the air conditioner where it was. I'm being transparent with this struggle because when designing studio apartments, you have to think outside the box.

For this space, I decided to turn Austen's bed around and conceal the unit by building a simple box out of plywood and attaching a door on hinges. This cover not only conceals the air conditioner, but also doubles as a side table! Using cane webbing on the front of the door means the air can still flow into the room. I used the loosest weave of cane webbing that I could find to maximize airflow. Enclosing the air conditioner also means that it's not visible at all when not in use for the many months of the year that it's not needed.

WHAT YOU'LL NEED

- Tape measure
- Sheet of ¾-inch (2 cm) plywood
- Circular saw
- Wood glue
- Wood screws
- Jigsaw
- Sandpaper
- Primer
- Paint in the color of your choice (use a latex paint in an eggshell, semigloss, or high-gloss finish)
- Two paintbrushes
- Two door hinges
- Two magnetic catches
- Cane webbing
- Staple gun
- Scissors
- Drill
- Decorative knob

Cord Management Ideas

A charging station will change the game. Find a multidevice organizer and never go scrambling for a charger again.

Install an under-the-desk cord tray, which holds a power bar, so you don't have ten cords hanging out under your workspace.

Invest in a light with a built-in charger to reduce the number of cords you have floating around.

Cord clips are inexpensive and the easiest way to keep your cords from falling behind your desk. (Is there anything more annoying?)

INSTRUCTIONS

1. Measure your air conditioner's height, width, and depth.

2. Add an additional 2 inches (5 cm) to each side of your measurements to account for the thickness of the plywood. Using these measurements, cut four pieces of plywood with a circular saw. You can rent this tool from the hardware store for one-off projects like this one.

3. Attach the sides together to create a box using wood glue and wood screws. The screws add more stability and keep the plywood from moving around, keeping the pieces together until the glue dries.

4. Measure the dimensions of the front opening and cut a piece for the door, subtracting ¼ inch from the width to account for the space needed to allow the door to open.

5. Cut out the window in the door using a jigsaw.

6. Sand the whole box, until you have a smooth finish on the edges and joints. Prime and then paint it.

7. Attach the hinges and two magnetic catches on the inside of the door, so that the door sits flush to the box.

8. Soak the cane webbing in water for 30 minutes. Using a staple gun (and an extra hand from another person), stretch the cane webbing across the back of the door while stapling along the perimeter of the door window. Cut away the excess webbing with scissors.

9. Drill a hole and install a decorative knob for a handle on the door front.

10. Place the completed box over your air conditioner unit and style your new side table! Note: If the box isn't sitting flush on top of your air conditioner or you're finding it's moving around, make sure you secure it for safety. You can do this by gluing a piece of wood to the top of the air conditioner and fastening the cover to the wood with wood screws. This isn't renter friendly, so make sure you get permission from your landlord first.

I used a small, square weave so that you wouldn't be able to see through the cane webbing and into the closet.

Snap and bring with you to shop!

HOW TO | Upgrade Closet Doors

I've seen many studio apartments in my day, and one of the most common ways landlords seem to cover closets is with curtains instead of doors. While I love this solution (I've definitely done this in makeovers, using a tension rod to make it renter friendly), you want to make sure that your curtains are the right length and not dragging on the floor. If the curtains are too short length- or width-wise, they aren't going to do a great job at hiding visual clutter. I also find when you have more than one closet, curtains used in this way can start to look a bit messy. And *especially* when you live in a studio apartment, creating as many closed-storage solutions as possible is key. So while I love this solution for a short-term rental, if you're looking for something a bit more substantial and decorative, then this DIY is for you!

> ## Psst
> *Installing new doors is usually a tricky process best left to the pros. It can take up to half a day or longer to get it right, and you actually have to chisel into the door frame to screw in hinges. But this DIY uses non-mortise hinges, which sit on the surface of your door and door frame, meaning you don't need to cut into any wood to install them.*

WHAT YOU'LL NEED

- Bi-folding closet doors (thrift these to save money—you can find lots secondhand)
- Hand saw
- Primer
- Paint
- Two paint rollers
- Cane webbing
- Staple gun
- Decorative knobs
- Non-mortise hinges
- Drill
- Drill bit

INSTRUCTIONS

1. You can either keep your doors as bi-folding, or take off the hinges with a drill like we've done here to create two separate panels for each closet. Now they open out instead of to the side.

2. Remove the slats that often come with bi-folding doors with a hand saw, leaving an opening.

3. Prime and then paint your doors with a paint roller.

4. Soak the cane webbing in water for 30 minutes. Using a staple gun (and an extra hand from another person), stretch the cane webbing across the back of the door while stapling along the perimeter of the door window. Cut away the excess with scissors.

5. Add trim to the back of the door around the cane webbing to prevent fraying and to keep it looking clean.

6. Add decorative knobs. If there are no pre-existing holes, you'll have to drill them first.

7. Install the doors to your door frame with a drill using non-mortise hinges, which are for surface mounting—meaning you don't have to chisel into your door frame.

Before You Move Out

I'M JUST GOING TO CUT TO THE CHASE: MOVING ISN'T
super fun, but it does signal a new beginning both for you and the space you are leaving. You've made this home your own and now it's time to pass it on to someone else, which means you may have to reverse some changes. This checklist will help make that process a little easier:

❏ Tenants who will move in after you might want to keep some of the changes you've made. Before you start reversing them, ask your landlord if you can get in touch with the people moving in and ask them if there's anything they'd like you to keep as is.

❏ Moving boxes are the *worst*. They're expensive, then used once and recycled. In a lot of cities, you can rent reusable plastic moving boxes that are delivered to your door and are returned after you're done with them. Plus, they're a more substantial option.

❏ Take down all of your artwork, hooks, and anything else that's made a hole in your walls. Spackle the holes left and paint over them. Have an electrician stop by for an hour to reinstall original fixtures. If you don't have the original lights anymore, there are tons of cheap ones you can buy at the hardware store for as little as twenty dollars.

❏ Same goes for knobs. Take your decorative ones with you for your next home and buy inexpensive ones as replacements, if you didn't keep the originals.

❏ If you have any paint left over, either bring it with you for your next home or leave it for the next tenants. Just make sure to clearly label which room each can of paint is for.

❏ For peel-and-stick tiles or backsplash that the next tenants don't want you to keep, remove it carefully with a hair dryer, as outlined on page 148.

Outro

SAYING GOODBYE TO

The Treehouse was one of the toughest things I've ever done. I dreaded the day I had to hand over my keys, because in a lot of ways, it felt way too soon to say goodbye after only two years there. At the same time, those two years were filled with big life changes. My career was taking off, I was in a loving, stable relationship, and The Treehouse had cradled me through some very tough times. Though it felt scary to let go of such a safe space, I knew the photos of that apartment would be documented in this book. When I look at them now, I see a home. And although it will be home to countless others as the years go by, in those moments and during that blip in time, there's no mistaking it belonged to me. That's the thing about design: It helps us claim these temporary or more permanent spaces as our own. It has the ability to make us feel safe and happy and is also always there for us when it feels like there's no other safe place around to land. Of course it's difficult to say goodbye. But the best part is once you hand over those keys, that means you can do it all over again in another space and make your mark, permanent or temporary—and hopefully with this book in tow.

Acknowledgments

WRITING A BOOK HAS BEEN A DREAM OF MINE SINCE
I was seven years old when I wrote my first story stapled together between two purple pieces of construction paper. But never, ever in my wildest-beyond-wild dreams did I think I would one day write a coffee-table book. Creating this has been an honor. The past four years have been a whirlwind, and every day I wake up filled with gratitude that this is the life I get to live because of the people who believe in me and this brand.

First and foremost, thank you to Team AG—Alana Andrade, Alessandra Sconza, Amanda Moroney, Carla Antonio, Graham Hayes, and James Resendes—for allowing me to live out my dream every day. My life is filled with so much joy because of the work we create together.

To my literary agent, Paige Sisley, for seeing something in me and making the dream I've had the longest come true. You've been my biggest champion from the beginning. Your insights, passion, guidance, and belief in me has made this book what it is.

To my team at Harper Design: Jenna Lefkowitz, my editor, and Shubhani Sarkar, designer, for allowing my vision for this book shine through so beautifully. And to Marta Schooler and Lynne Yeamans for being so excited and invested in this book. You've made this process incredibly rewarding.

To Rayna Schwartz, for all your hard work producing this book and making my ideas come to life. You have such a gift for making everything you touch look so beautiful. I couldn't have done it without you.

To Lauren Kolyn—I knew as soon as the idea for this book was born your images had to illustrate it. You bring my interiors to life in such a special way, and I'm honored your work is a part of it.

To Alanna Chelmick, for making me feel like the best version of myself and for accepting the fact that I will never let you use hairspray. I'm very grateful to have you in my corner.

Thank you to my family at Kin Community. Your abiding belief in me since the beginning has created so many amazing opportunities in my career.

Thank you to Amanda Moroney, my biggest champion and confidant, for continuing to push me to do bigger and better things. You are one of the most talented in this industry, and I couldn't imagine doing this without you by my side. You make all the dreams that I have attainable, like writing this book. Your ability to be the sharpest businesswoman around while also caring for everyone on the team so lovingly is a skill that I admire in you so much.

To Carla Antonio, for being with me since day one and encouraging me to start my own YouTube channel. There is so much of this journey that wouldn't have existed without you. Over the last four years, you have made me feel comfortable being myself on camera, and I have grown so much because of your guidance and direction. Thank you for making the spaces I design look so beautiful in every single video you shoot. Our friendship means so much to me.

To Alana Andrade, my creative twin flame, for being here since the very beginning. I can't wait to see all the amazing things we will continue to create together.

To Christina, for being a safe place to land when it felt like the ground beneath me wasn't so soft.

To my aunt Samantha and mom, Virginia, for being my biggest cheerleaders and equally loving critics. To the rest of my family—my dad, Chris, my sister, Olivia, Mark and Debs, Eva, and, of course, Noah, for the endless and unwavering support.

And to my viewers: Without you tuning in every week, none of this would be possible. Thank you for engaging in my content, for your positive comments and messages and your hellos in the streets. It means more to me than you'll ever know. I love creating content for you and I hope it is something I get to continue to do for years to come.

Shopping Credits

Cover: Sofa, ikea.com. Sofa cover, bemz.com. Sofa legs, prettypegs.com. Caramel throw pillow, soccoliving.ca. Plaid throw pillows tonicliving.com. Raffia textured throw pillow, shopcasa chic.ca. Beige fringe throw pillow, hm.com. Lumbar cream throw pillow, shophacienda.com. Rug, wayfair.com. Slippers, alexandragater.com. Art, emilykeatingsnyder.com.

Page 1: Paint (Mascarpone), benjamin moore.com. Floating nightstand, article.com. Round throw pillow, urbanoutfitters.com. Framed wallpaper, etsy.com/shop/tropicwall. Nightstand art, iamfy.co. Rug, rugsusa.com. Floating bookshelves, umbra.com. Slippers, shop.verloopknits.com. Side light, casper.com.

Pages 2–3: Navy patterned throw pillow, green throw pillow, black side table, floor lamp, grey and cream poufs, patterned rug, navy console, decorative knot, large floor vases, wooden knot, rattan table, cream dotted rug, homesense.ca. Mint vase, bud vases, pink vase, eq3.com. Terra-cotta armchair, pouf stool, table lamp, vdevmaison.com. Velvet gold throw pillow, tonicliving.com. Lacquer trays, pedestal planter, indigo.com. Fluted table, westelm.com. Pink chair, gusmodern.com. Pink throw pillow, hm.com. Black chair, article.com. All artwork, iamfy.co.

Page 5: Frame TV, samsung.com. Chair, shopcasachic.ca. Rug, qalat.ca. Art on tv, etsy.com/shop/VividDigital Art. Wood side tables, justbewoodsy .com. Table lamp, anthropologie.com. Mounted wall light, cb2.com. Planter, bouclair.com. Black frames, opposite wall.com. Oversized mattes in frames, custommat.ca Pom-pom basket, baba souk.ca. Candles, kinsfolkshop.com. Console table, custom made piece.

Page 8: Navy console, large vase, rattan table, wooden knot, cream pouf, homesense.ca. Velvet pouf stool, vdev maison.com. Mint vase, bud vases, eq3.com. Table lamp, vdevmaison.com. Fluted table, westelm.com. Velvet gold throw pillow, tonicliving.com. Pink chair, gusmodern.com. Rug, hm.com.

Page 11: Pink plates, fable.com. Napkins, maisontess.com. Stemmed glassware, indigo.com. Cutlery, anthropologie.com. Handle pitcher, zarahome.com. Other pitcher, ikea .com. Fresh flowers, euclidfarms.com. Chair, article.com.

Page 12: Paint (Coffee Cream), pure-original.com. Wood wall art,

katiegong.com. Bedframe, underbed storage, article.com. Black throw pillow, soccoliving.ca. Lumbar throw pillow, shophacienda.com. Black and white and mint throw pillows, hm.com. Bedding, shopdreams jumper.com. Side tables, etsy.com /shop/MoniWoodCo. Side light, casper.com.

Page 16: Fabric swatches, tonicliving .com. Gold tile, cletile.com. Square squiggle tile, colored tiles, fireclaytile .com. Cane webbing, levairscaning supplies.ca. Beaded garland, amazon. ca. Fan knob, etsy.com/shop/haode sign. Gold knob, amazon.com.

Page 19: Paint (Modern Love), back drophome.com. Desk chair, theapart mentlife.ca. Floating shelf, floating desk, Pegboard, ikea.com. Closet light, amazon.com.

Page 20: Frame TV, samsung.com. Art on TV, Following The Pack by Jennifer Daily, minted.com. Design sandwich print, alexandragater. com. Floating shelf, ikea.com. Heart art, banquetworkshop.com. Rug, rugsusa.com. Pink power art print, society6.com. As If art print, theprint ableconcept.com. Yellow rainbow print, emilykeatingsnyder.com. Console table, custom made piece. Baskets, gold candle holder, target .com. Coral armchair, article.com

Page 22: Paint (Artichoke), benjamin moore.com. Karlstad sofa, ikea.com. Sofa cover, legs, bemz.com. Rug, rugs usa.com. Candleholder, homesense.ca. Side table, bedbathandbeyond.com. Art, etsy.com/shop/JennKitagawa. Striped throw pillows, hm.com.

Page 27: Paint (Simply White and Windsor Green), benjaminmoore .com. Pendant light, shopcasachic.ca. Art prints, iamfy.co. Wall basket, amazon.com. Rug, rugsusa.com. Mirror, wayfair.com. Table runner, cb2.com. Napkins, target.com. Vase, indigo.com. Dried flowers, bespoke blossoms.com.

Page 28: Karlstad sofa, ikea.com. Sofa cover, bemz.com. Frame TV, samsung .com. Chair, shopcasachic.ca. Rug, qalat.ca. Wood side tables, justbewoodsy .com. Art on TV, etsy.com/shop/Vivid DigitalArt. Table lamp, anthropologie .com. Mounted wall light, cb2.com. Planter, bouclair.com. Console table, custom made piece. Black frames, oppositewall.com. Oversized mattes in frames, custommat.ca. Pom-pom basket, babasouk.ca. Candles, kinsfolk shop.com. Polka dot throw pillow, etsy.com/shop/TownsendRoweHome. Purple floor pouf, theboholab.com.

Page 30: Geometric art, juniper printshop.com. Palm tree art, iamfy .co. Floor lamp, article.com. Dresser,

pulls, ikea.com. Legs, beaded garland, amazon.com. Vase, thrifted. Flower art, minted.com.

Page 32: Countertop, sink, faucet, jars, ikea.com. Paint and primer (Dragonfly), benjaminmoore.com. Backsplash, thesmarttiles.com. Knobs and drawer pulls, cb2.com. Wallpaper, livetteswallpaper.com. Light, mitzi.com. Dishtowel, halihalidesign.com.

Page 35: Chairs, shopcasachic.ca. Chair cushions, hm.com. Bird cage pendant, etsy.com. Wall sconce, colorcord.com. Vase, hm.com. Table, thrifted.

Page 36: Pomegranate salt and pepper shakers, anthropologie.com. Peel-and-stick backsplash, thesmarttiles.com. Counter, lowes.ca. Sink, ikea.com. Knobs, cb2.com. Faucet, homedepot .ca. Utensil jug, Gold measuring cups, target.com. Dish brush, Amber soap dispenser, amazon.com. Dotted soap dispenser, homesense.ca. Drying rack, cb2.com.

Page 38: Tiles, fireclaytile.com. Cane webbing, levairscaningsupplies.ca. Oversized pom-pom tassel, etsy.com /shop/XinhandcoGoods.

Page 39: Art prints, iamfy.co. Table runner, cb2.com. Napkins, target.com. Vase, indigo.com. Dried flowers bespokeblossoms.com

Pages 40–41: Fabric swatches, tonic living.com. Gold tile, cletile.com. Square squiggle tile, colored tiles, fireclaytile .com. Cane webbing, levairscaning supplies.ca. Beaded garland, amazon.ca. Fan knob, etsy.com/shop/haodesign. Gold knob, amazon.com.

Pages 42–43: Navy patterned throw pillow, green throw pillow, black side table, floor lamp, grey and cream poufs, rug, navy console, decorative knot, large floor vases, rattan table, wooden knot, cream dotted rug, hanging light, homesense.ca. Mint vase, bud vases on rattan table, pink vase, eq3.com. Terra-cotta arm chair, velvet pouf stool, table lamp, vdevmaison.com. Velvet gold throw pillow, tonicliving.com. Lacquer trays, pedestal planter, indigo.com. Fluted table, westelm.com. Pink chair, gusmodern.com. Pink throw pillow, hm.com. Black chair, article.com. All artwork, iamfy.co.

Page 45: Karlstad sofa, ikea.com. Sofa cover, sofa legs, bemz.com. Chair, shopcasachic.ca. Rug, qalat.ca. Wood side tables, justbewoodsy.com. Table lamp, anthropologie.com. Mounted wall light, cb2.com. Ivar cabinet, ikea .com. Paint (Pigeon), farrow-ball.com. Cane webbing, levairscaningsupplies .ca. Candleholder, hm.com. Art, jenniferament.com. Dried flowers and planter, homesense.ca. Polka

dot throw pillow, etsy.com/shop /TownsendRoweHome.

Page 46: Floor lamp, plant and basket, decorative knot, homesense.ca. Terra-cotta armchair, velvet pouf stool, vdevmaison.com. Lacquer tray, indigo.com. Throw pillow, hm.com. Rug, hm.com.

Page 47: Chair, shopcasachic.ca. Seat cushion pillow, hm.com. Rug, navy console, plant and basket, homesense .ca. Vases, eq3.com. Lacquer tray, indigo.com. Artwork, desenio.com

Page 48: Plant and basket, floor vase, side table, wooden knot, table lamp, rug, homesense.ca. Throw pillow, tonic living.com. Pink chair, gusmodern.com.

Page 49: Plant and basket, rattan table, table vase, rug, homesense. ca. Throw pillows, hm.com. Pedestal planter, indigo.com. Framed wall-paper, dropitmodern.com. Frames, oppositewall.com. Chair, article.com

Page 57: Floating shelf, ikea.com. Vases, eq3.com. Crane artwork, desenio.com, Other artwork, iamfy.co.

Page 59: Artwork, super-rural.com. Jug, homesense.ca.

Pages 62–63: Circle paint (Allspice), benjaminmoore.com. Pendant light, shopcasachic.ca. Bed, ikea.com. Throw pillows, target.com. Swan, homesense.ca.

Pages 68–69: Wallpaper, dropit modern.com.

Page 74: Paint (Coffee Cream), pure-original.com. Wood wall art, katiegong.com. Bedframe, underbed storage, article.com. Black throw pillow, soccoliving.ca. Lumbar throw pillow, shophacienda.com. Black and white and mint throw pillows, hm.com. Bedding, shopdreams jumper.com. Side light, casper.com. Runner, mellah.ca. Ceiling light, hay .com. Slippers, alexandragater.com. Framed art, emilykeatingsnyder.com. Vase, thrifted.

Page 77: Vase art, etsy.com/shop /modeaprints. Abstract Art, etsy.com /shop/Wartdesignstudio. Vase and planter, homesense.ca. Candleholder, hm.com.

Page 78: Art, emilykeatingsnyder.com. Vase, hm.com.

Page 81: Salt and pepper grinders, finnishdesignshop.com. Jug, home sense.ca. Table lamp, soccoliving.ca.

Page 82: Paint (Coffee Cream), pure-original.com. Wood wall art, katiegong.com. Bedframe, article .com. Side tables, etsy.com/shop /MoniWoodCo. Side light, casper.com. Framed art, emilykeatingsnyder.com. Vase,thrifted. Stool,structube.com.

Page 89: Paint (Salamander), benjamin moore.com. Bench, thrifted. Wall hook, amazon.com.

Page 90: Paint (Fresco Lime), bergs maspaint.com. Headboard, expansion pieces, article.com. Pendant light, knowltonandco.co. Mirror, etsy .com/shop/MirrorHomeDecorArt. Candleholder, hm.com.

Page 91: Shelves, ikea.com.

Page 92: Paint (Regent Green), benjaminmoore.com. Desk, article.com. Desk chair, westelm.com. Clock, staples.com. Table vase, bouclair.com. Circle vase, hm.com. Floating shelf, cb2.com. Art on shelf, society6.com. Art above bed, desenio.com. Desk light, anthropologie.com.

Pages 94–95: Wallpaper, etsy.com /shop/xwallcolors. Shelf, light switch plates, amazon.com. Soap dish, candle, vdevmaison.com. Candleholder, thrifted. Mirror, thrifted.

Page 96: Wallpaper, dropitmodern.com.

Page 97: Wall decals, etsy.com/ca /shop/LUMAwallsdecor.

Page 99: Raffia basket, babasouk.ca. Mirror, ikea.com. Light, amazon.com. Basket, target.com.

Pages 100–101: Raffia basket, baba souk.ca. Mirror, ikea.com. Light, amazon.com. Basket, target.com.

Page 102: Art prints, iamfy.co. Wall basket, amazon.com. Circle wall vase, urbanoutfitters.com.

Page 103: Mirror, Cabinet, ikea.com.

Page 104: Circle vase, hm.com. Floating shelf, cb2.com. Artwork, society6.com.

Page 105: Art on TV, etsy.com/shop /VividDigitalArt.com. Frame TV, samsung.com. Design sandwich print, alexandragater.com. Art on tv, Following The Pack by Jennifer Daily, minted .com. Floating shelf, ikea.com. Black typography art, tgoodman.com. Pink typography art, society6.com. Rainbow art, emilykeatingsnyder.com. Console table, custom made piece. Candleholder, target.com.

Page 106: Pink and black fabric, minted.com. Dotted wallpaper, dropit modern.com. Black and white affirmation cards, noteandshine.co.uk/. Frames, oppositewall.com. Purple and mustard sponge cloth, halihali.com.

Page 108: (top) Paint (Coffee Cream), pure-original.com. Wood wall art, katiegong.com. Bedframe, article .com. Black throw pillow, soccoliving .ca. Lumbar throw pillow, shophaci enda.com. Black and white and mint throw pillows, hm.com. Bedding,

shopdreamsjumper.com. Side tables, etsy.com/shop/MoniWoodCo. Side lights, casper.com. (bottom) Paint (Coffee Cream), pure-original.com. Hanging rug, babasouk.ca. Bedframe, article.com. Camel throw pillows, soccoliving.ca. Polka dot and pink throw pillows, simons.ca. Bedding, shopdreamsjumper.com. Side tables, etsy.com/shop/MoniWoodCo. Side lights, casper.com.

Page 109: (top) Paint (Coffee Cream), pure-original.com. Dried floral arrangement, etsy.com/shop/shop goldenaugust. Bedframe, article.com. Throw pillows, soccoliving.ca. Lumbar throw pillow, shophacienda.com. Bedding, shopdreamsjumper.com. Side tables, etsy.com/shop/MoniWoodCo. Side lights, casper.com. (bottom) Paint (Coffee Cream), pure-original .com. Rope wall hanging, candiceluter .ca. Bedframe, article.com. Throw pillows, hm.com. Bedding, shop dreamsjumper.com. Side tables, etsy .com/shop/MoniWoodCo. Side lights, casper.com.

Page 111: (Mustard wrapping paper, cyanotypepaper.com. Dotted wall-paper, dropitmodern.com. Black and pink fabric, minted.com. Greeting cards, juxtaposehome.ca. Frames, oppositewall.com. Custom mats, custommat.ca. Terracotta armchair, vdevmaison.com. Circle throw pillow, hm.com. Small blue affirmation cards, peopleiveloved.com. Orange affirma-tion cards, Phoebe Taylor. Black and white affirmation cards, noteandshine .co.uk/. Sponge cloth, halihali.com.

Page 112: (top left) Wallpaper, dropit modern.com. Fabric, minted.com. Greeting cards, juxtaposehome.ca. Frames, oppositewall.com. Custom mats, custommat.ca. (top right) Wrapping paper, cyanotypepaper.com. Frames, oppositewall.com. Custom mats, custommat.ca. Small affirmation cards, peopleiveloved.com. (bottom left) Frames, oppositewall.com. Custom mats, custommat.ca. (bottom right) Frames, oppositewall.com. Custom mats, custommat.ca. Black and white affirmation cards, noteandshine.co.uk/. Sponge cloth, halihali.com.

Page 113: Large art, alexandragater .com. Rainbow art, emilykeating synder.com. People hugging art, peopleiveloved.com

Page 114: Chandelier, mitzi.com. Dining table, article.com. Dining chairs, shopcasachic.ca. Dried bouquet, bespokeblossoms.com. Astrology print, instagram.com/queenofwhines. Planter, commonhousestudio.ca.

Page 115: Frame TV, samsung.com. Art on tv, etsy.com/shop/VividDigital

Art. Chair, shopcasachic.ca. Wood side tables, justbewoodsy.com. Table lamp, anthropologie.com. Mounted wall light, cb2.com. Basket with lid, babasouk.ca. Polka dot throw pillow, etsy.com/shop/TownsendRoweHome. Console table, custom made piece. Black frames, oppositewall.com. Over-sized mattes in frames, custommat .ca. Pom-pom basket, babasouk.ca. Candles, kinsfolkshop.com. Polka dot throw pillow, etsy.com/shop /TownsendRoweHome. Purple floor pouf, theboholab.com.

Page 118: Art on TV, etsy.com/shop/ VividDigitalArt.com. Frame TV, sam sung.com. Lamp, anthropologie.com. Art on tv, etsy.com/shop/VividDigital Art. Basket planter, babasouk.ca.

Page 120: Bedding, urbanoutfitters .com. Lamp, etsy.com. Side table, bedbathandbeyond.com. Headboard, custom made piece.

Page 121: Chair, shopcasachic.ca. Wall light, cb2.com. Basket with lid, baba souk.ca. Polka dot throw pillow, etsy .com/shop/TownsendRoweHome.

Page 122: Headboard, article.com. Bedframe, ikea.com. Floating book-shelves, umbra.com. Stool, homesense .ca. Rug, rugsusa.com. Check throw pillow, simons.ca. Door paint (Rasp-berry Ice), benjaminmoore.com. Cane webbing, levairscaningsupplies.ca. Squiggle handles, urbanoutfitters.com. Bedding, shopflaxhome.com.

Page 125: Headboard, instagram .com/makemovesvintage. Pendant light, ikea.com. Curtains, Bedding, urbanoutfitters.com. Curtain rod, umbra.com. Lumbar pillow, target .com. Quilt, wayfair.com.

Page 126–127: Sofa, ikea.com. Sofa cover, bemz.com. Sofa legs, prettypegs .com. Caramel throw pillow, soccoliving .ca. Plaid throw pillow, tonicliving.com. Raffia textured throw pillow, shopcasa chic.ca. Beige fringe throw pillow, hm.com. Lumbar cream throw pillow, shophacienda.com. Rug, wayfair.com. Slippers, alexandragater.com. Art, emilykeatingsnyder.com. Pink plant pot, commonhousestudio.ca.

Page 128: (top) Sofa, ikea.com. Sofa cover, bemz.com. Sofa legs, pretty pegs.com. Caramel throw pillow, soccoliving.ca. Plaid throw pillow, tonicliving.com. Raffia textured throw pillow, shopcasachic.ca. Beige fringe throw pillow, hm.com. Lumbar cream throw pillow, shophacienda.com. Rug, wayfair.com. Art, emilykeatingsnyder .com. Wood side table, justbewoodsy .com. (bottom) Sofa, ikea.com. Sofa cover, bemz.com. Sofa legs, prettypegs .com. Blue and blue shapes throw pil-lows, indigo.com. Shapes throw pillow,

westelm.com. Abstract shapes throw pillow, shophacienda.com. Round throw pillow, crateandbarrel.ca. Rug, rugsusa.com. Art, emilykeatingsnyder .com. Wood side table, justbewoodsy .com. Table vase, bouclair.com.

Page 129: (top) Sofa, ikea.com. Sofa cover, bemz.com. Sofa legs, prettypegs .com. Mudcloth throw pillow, baba souk.ca. Sage throw pillow, hm.com Black and white texture throw pillow, mumotoronto.com. Charcoal over-sized throw pillow, soccoliving.ca. Circle throw pillow, shophacienda.com. Faces throw pillow, society6.com. Rug, wayfair.com. Art, emilykeatingsnyder .com. Wood side table, justbewoodsy .com. Table vase, hm.com. (bottom) Sofa, ikea.com. Sofa cover, bemz.com. Sofa legs, bemz.com. Lilac throw pillow, hm.com. Green throw pillow, bouclair.com. Blue velvet throw pillow, tonicliving.com. Triangle throw pillow, indigo.com. Throw blanket, soccoliving.ca. Purple triangle design throw pillow, mumotoronto.com. Gray throw pillow, hm.com. Rug, rugsusa .com. Art, emilykeatingsnyder.com. Wood side table, justbewoodsy.com.

Page 130: Paint (Graphite), benjamin moore.com. Planter, anthropologie .com. Lacquer tray, indigo.com. Malm side table, ikea.com. Fronts, norse interiors.com. Pulls, etsy.com/shop /FUTERAL. Bedding, hm.com.

Page 131: Pax wardrobes, ikea.com. Custom MDF wardrobe fronts, nieucabinetdoors.com. Orange rug, rugsusa.com. Wavy cabinet door handles, urbanoutfitters.com. Mint green ladder, wayfair.com. Pom-pom basket, babasouk.ca.

Page 133: Dish rack, oyoylivingdesign .com. Dishcloths, tenandco.ca. Dish brush, amazon.com. Andree Jardin dust pan and brush, smallable.com. Garden hose, gardenglory.com. Step-ladder, wayfair.com. Garbage can, bra bantia.com. Salt and pepper shakers, finnishdesignshop.com. S-hook, etsy .com/shop/brighttia. Reusable straws, etsy.com/shop/kessellate. Clothing hangers, amazon.com. Wall hooks, fermliving.com. Trivets, halihali.com. Exposed lightbulb, cb2.com.

Page 134: Green paint (Pigeon), farrow-ball.com. Hexagon knobs, cb2 .com. Semicircle drawer pulls, etsy .com/shop/GorgeousDesignHome. Tiles, riadtile.com. Egg holder, kinsfolkshop.com. Compost bin, wooden boards, homesense.ca. Bowls, plates, shophacienda.com. Raffia basket, babasouk.ca. Ceramic mugs, sugarhouseceramicco.com. Colored stem glassware, indigo.com. Olive oil, pineapplecollaborative.com. Pink rainbow trivet, funsty.ca. Pomegranate salt and pepper shakers, anthropologie.com. Art, desenio.com.

Page 137: Paint (Salamander), benjaminmoore.com. Wallpaper, livettes wallpaper.com. Chair, article.com.

Page 138: Artwork, deborahmargo.com. Stair runner, wayfair.com. Planter, homesense.ca. Watering can, target.com.

Pages 140–141: Pomegranate salt and pepper shakers, anthropologie.com. Peel-and-stick backsplash, thesmarttiles.com. Counter, lowes.ca. Sink, ikea.com. Knobs, cb2.com. Faucet, homedepot.ca. Utensil jug, Gold measuring cups, target.com. Dish brush, amber soap dispenser, amazon.com. Dotted soap dispenser, homesense.com. Drying rack, cb2.com.

Pages 142–143: Green paint (Bancha), farrow-ball.com. Peel-and-stick backsplash, quadrostyle.com. Knobs, amazon.com. Yellow low bowls and black bowls, indigo.com. Jars, ikea.com. Coffee machine, breville.com. Olive oil, pineapplecollaborative.com. Lemon salt and pepper shakers, vdevmaison.com. Lamp, thrifted. Fruit bowl, virginiasin.com. Tea towel, maisontess.com.

Page 144: (top right) Green paint (Bancha), farrow-ball.com. Peel-and-stick backsplash, quadrostyle.com. Knobs, amazon.com. Lamp, thrifted. Fruit bowl, virginiasin.com. (bottom left) Green paint (Bancha), farrow-ball.com. Peel-and-stick backsplash, quadrostyle.com. Knobs, amazon.com. Rug, soccoliving.ca. Fruit bowl, virginiasin.com. Tea towel, maisontess.com. (bottom right) Green paint (Bancha), farrow-ball.com. Peel-and-stick backsplash, quadrostyle.com. Knobs, amazon.com. Yellow low bowls and black bowls, indigo.com. Jars, ikea.com.

Page 145: (top) Green paint (Bancha), farrow-ball.com. Knobs, amazon.com. Pot rail, floating shelf, ikea.com. Apple cider vinegar, pineapplecollaborative.com. Artwork, bellwoodsbrewery.com. Pom-pom tea towel, halihalidesign.com. Fruit bowl, virginiasin.com. Tea towel, maisontess.com. Lamp, thrifted. (bottom left) Apple cider vinegar, pineapplecollaborative.com. Artwork, bellwoodsbrewery.com. (bottom right) Peel-and-stick backsplash, quadrostyle.com. Olive oil, pineapplecollaborative.com. Lemon salt and pepper shakers, vdevmaison.com.

Page 147: Peel-and-stick backsplash, thesmarttiles.com.

Pages 148–149: Peel-and-stick backsplash, thesmarttiles.com. Counter, lowes.ca. Sink, ikea.com. Knobs, cb2.com. Faucet, homedepot.ca. Jars, ikea.com. French press, lecreuset.com. Amber soap dispenser, amazon.com. Dotted soap dispenser, homesense.ca. Pulls, anthropologie.com. Planter basket, target.com.

Pages 150: (top) Fruit bowl, indigo.com. (bottom) Compost bin and wooden boards, homesense.ca. Pink glasses, ikea.com.

Page 151: Green paint (Pigeon), farrow-ball.com. Hexagon knobs, cb2.com. Semicircle drawer pulls, etsy.com/shop/GorgeousDesignHome. Tiles, riadtile.com. Pinks bowls and plates, shop hacienda.com. Raffia basket, babasouk.ca. White plates, fable.com. Ceramic mugs, sugarhouseceramicco.com. Olive oil, pineapplecollaborative.com. Pomegranate salt and pepper shakers, anthropologie.com. Colored stemware, indigo.com. Compost bin and wooden boards, homesense.ca. Curtain, etsy.com/shop/BicoEstonia. Bird light, etsy.com. Tea towel, urbanoutfitters.com. Face artwork, desenio.com. Heart artwork, banquetworkshop.com. Fruit bowl, indigo.com. Chairs, stowedhome.com. Pom-pom basket, babasouk.ca. Rattan tray, homesense.ca. Runner, westelm.com.

Page 152: (top) Plates, fable.com. Raffia basket, babasouk.ca. Artwork, desenio.com. Bowls, fable.com. Flower scissors, vdevmaison.com. (bottom) Green paint (Pigeon), farrow-ball.com. Hexagon knobs, cb2.com. Salt and pepper grinders, finnishdesignshop.com. Egg holder, kinsfolkshop.com. Table lamp, soccoliving.ca. Utensil jug, target.com. Oven mitt, halihalidesign.com.

Page 153: (top) Compost bin, homesense.ca. Tea towel, shophacienda.com. Curtain, etsy.com/shop/BicoEstonia. Polka dot cushion, etsy.com/shop/TownsendRoweHome. Terra-cotta throw pillow, soccoliving.ca. Round throw pillow, beige pola dot throw pillow, hm.com. Semicircle drawer pulls, etsy.com/shop/GorgeousDesignHome. Art, banquetworkshop.com. Pink glasses, ikea.com. (bottom left) Pink plates, napkins, brush, shophacienda.com. White plates, fable.com. Sponge dish, babasouk.ca. Tiles, riadtile.com. (bottom right) Chairs, stowedhome.com. Pom-pom basket, babasouk.ca. Rattan tray, homesense.ca. Runner, westelm.com.

Page 156: Green paint (Pigeon), farrow-ball.com. Hexagon knobs, cb2.com. Semicircle drawer pulls, etsy.com/shop/GorgeousDesignHome. Tiles, riadtile.com. Pinks plates, napkins, tea towel, shophacienda.com. Dish sponges, shophacienda.com. White plates, fable.com. Sponge dish, raffia basket, babasouk.ca. Compost bin and wooden boards, homesense.ca.

Ceramic mugs, sugarhouseceramicco.com. Olive oil, pineapplecollaborative.com. Pink rainbow trivet, funsty.ca. Pomegranate salt and pepper shakers, anthropologie.com. Colored stemware, indigo.com. Artwork, desenio.com.

Page 157: Paint and primer (Dragonfly), benjaminmoore.com. Hexagon knobs, cb2.com. Jars, ikea.com.

Pages 158–159: Paint and primer (Dragonfly), benjaminmoore.com. Countertop, sink, faucet, jars, ikea.com. Backsplash, thesmarttiles.com. Knobs and drawer pulls, cb2.com. Tea towel, halihalidesign.com.

Page 160: (top) Art, minted.com. (bottom) Countertop, sink, faucet, jars, ikea.com.

Page 161: (top) Paint and primer (Dragonfly), benjaminmoore.com. Countertop, sink, faucet, jars, ikea.com. Backsplash, thesmarttiles.com. Knobs and drawer pulls, cb2.com. Art, minted.com. Wallpaper, livetteswallpaper.com. Light, mitzi.com. (bottom left) Jars, ikea.com. Drawer pulls, cb2.com. Tea towel, halihalidesign.com. (bottom right) Art, minted.com. Jars, ikea.com. Backsplash, thesmarttiles.com.

Page 163: Paint and primer (Dragonfly), benjaminmoore.com.

Page 164: Peel-and-stick backsplash, thesmarttiles.com. Counter, lowes.ca. Knobs, cb2.com. Jars, ikea.com. French press, lecreuset.com. Pulls, anthropologie.com. Planter basket, rug, target.com.

Page 166: Jars, ikea.com.

Page 167: Shelves, brackets, jars, spice jars, white bins, ikea.com. Wallpaper, livetteswallpaper.com. Ceramic baskets, urbanoutfitters.com. Olive oil, pineapplecollaborative.com. Salt and pepper grinders, finnishdesignshop.com. Chalk labels, amazon.com.

Pages 168–169: Paint (Coffee Cream), pure-original.com. Wood wall art, katiegong.com. Bedframe, article.com. Black throw pillow, soccoliving.ca. Black and white and mint throw pillows, hm.com. Bedding, shopdreamsjumper.com. Side tables, etsy.com/shop/MoniWoodCo. Side lights, casper.com. Planter, sugarhouseceramicco.com.

Pages 170–171: Paint (Graphite), benjaminmoore.com. Planter, anthropologie.com. Lacquer tray, indigo.com. Malm side table, ikea.com. Fronts, norseinteriors.com. Pulls, etsy.com/shop/FUTERAL. Bed, article.com. Light, cb2.com. Bedding, throw pillows, hm.com. Custom canvas, posterjack.ca. Digital artwork, juniperprintshop.com.

Page 172: (bottom left) Art, minted.com. Handles, amazon.com. (top) Paint (Graphite), benjaminmoore.com. Bed, article.com. Bedding, throw pillows, hm.com. Custom canvas, posterjack.ca. Digital artwork, juniperprintshop.com. Curtains, westelm.com. Curtain pulls, anthropologie.com. (bottom right) Jewelry tray, westelm, com. Tissue box, mouchehome.com

Page 173: (top) Paint (Graphite), benjaminmoore.com. Bed, pendant light, article.com. Bedding, throw pillows, hm.com. Custom canvas, posterjack.ca. Digital artwork, juniperprintshop.com. Light, cb2.com. Pom-pom tassel, etsy.com/shop/Xinhandcogoods. (bottom left) Curtains, westelm.com. Curtain pulls, anthropologie.com. (bottom right) Malm side table, ikea.com. Fronts, norseinteriors.com. Pulls, etsy.com/shop/FUTERAL.

Page 175: Paint (Graphite), benjaminmoore.com. Side table, westelm.com. Bed, article.com. Custom canvas, juniperprintshop.com. Rug, rugsusa.com. Oversized throw pillows, Beige textured duvet cover, hm.com. Sheets, somnhome.com. Peach duvet cover, shopdreamsjumper.com. Quilt, shopflaxhome.com. Textured throw pillow, babasouk.ca.

Page 176: Handles, amazon.com.

Page 178: Wallpaper, tempaper.com. Hangers, amazon.com.

Page 179: (top left) Wallpaper, tempaper.com. Baskets, ikea.com. Hangers, amazon.com. (top right) Wallpaper, tempaper.com. Hamper, grid hanging storage, amazon.com. (bottom left) Floor light, target.com. Hangers, Clothing rack, amazon.com.. (bottom right) Underbed storage, article.com. Throw blankets, hm.com.

Page 180: Dresser, ikea.com. Knobs, vdevmaison.com. Mirror, structube.com. Hanging planter, smallhours.ca. Floor planter, homesense.ca.

Page 181: Bar cart, ikea.com.

Pages 182–183: Paint (Mascarpone), benjaminmoore.com. Floating nightstands, article.com. Candles and candleholders, cb2.com. Round throw pillow, urbanoutfitters.com. Square throw pillow, hm.com. Framed wallpaper, etsy.com/shop/tropicwall. Bedside art, iamfy.co. Side lights, casper.com.

Page 184: (bottom left) Curtain rod, anthropologie.com. Curtain, hm.com. (top) Floating nightstand, article.com. Candles and candleholders, cb2.com. Side lights, casper.com. (bottom right) Dresser, ikea.com. Knobs, vdevmaison.com. Hanging planter, smallhours.ca.

Floor planter, wayfair.com. Hanging bead tassel, amazon.com. Mirror, structube.com.

Page 185: (top) Floating nightstand, article.com. Art, iamfy.co. Throw blanket, round throw pillow, urban outfitters.com. Rug, rugsusa.com. Side light, casper.com. Slippers, shop .verloopknits.com. (bottom left) Framed Wallpaper, etsy.com/shop /tropicwall. (bottom right) Floating book shelves, umbra.com.

Pages 186–187: Headboard, insta gram.com/makemovesvintage. Curtains, Bedding, urbanoutfitters .com. Curtain rod, umbra.com. Lumbar pillow, target.com. Pink pillows, wayfair.com. Lights, amazon.com.

Page 188: (bottom left) Pendant light, ikea.com. (top) Dresser, thrifted. Lamp target.com. (bottom right) Headboard, instagram.com/makemovesvintage. Curtains, bedding, urbanoutfitters .com. Curtain rod, umbra.com. Lights, amazon.com.

Page 189: (top) Eye mirror, baba souk.ca. (bottom left) Planter, homesense.ca. (bottom right) Hand, homesense.ca.

Page 191: Headboard, instagram.com /makemovesvintage, Curtains, Bedding, urbanoutfitters.com. Curtain rod, umbra.com. Lumbar pillow, target.com. Pink pillows, wayfair.com. Lights, amazon.com.

Page 192: Frame TV, samsung.com. Chair, shopcasachic.ca. Wood side table, justbewoodsy.com. Table lamp, anthropologie.com. Planter, bouclair .com. Console table, custom made piece. Black frames, oppositewall.com. Oversized mattes in frames, custom mat.ca Pom-pom basket, babasouk.ca. Candles, kinsfolkshop.com. Slippers, alexandragater.com.

Pages 194–195: Paint (Artichoke), benjaminmoore.com. Rug, rugsusa .com. Floor lamp, coffee table, candle-holder, fur throw, homesense.ca. Side table, bedbathandbeyond.com. Art, etsy.com/shop/JennKitagawa. Striped throw pillows, hm.com. Karlstad sofa, ikea.com. Sofa cover, legs, bemz.com.

Page 196: Armchairs, article.com. Kallax shelves, baskets, ikea.com. Legs, bemz.com. Pet bed, homesense.ca.

Page 197: (top left) Armchair, article .com. Ceiling fan, homedepot.com. Pet bed, homesense.ca. Mirror, thrifted. Throw blanket, homesense.ca. (top right) Bar cart, homesense.ca. Art print, sidedimes.com. (bottom left) Side table, bedbathandbeyond.com. Art, etsy.com/shop/JennKitagawa. Candleholder, homesense.ca. Striped throw pillows, hm.com. Karlstad sofa,

ikea.com. Sofa cover, legs, bemz.com. (bottom right) Floor lamp, article. com. Striped throw pillow, hm.com. Curtains, ikea.com.

Page 199: (top) Karlstad sofa, ikea .com. Sofa cover, bemz.com. Rug, rugsusa.com. White Throw pillow, tonicliving.com. Green and pink lumbar pillows, target.com. Orange throw pillow, indigo.com. Sofa legs, prettypegs.com. (bottom) Karlstad sofa, ikea.com. Sofa cover, bemz .com. Chair, shopcasachic.ca. Polka dot throw pillow, etsy.com/shop /TownsendRoweHome. Wood side tables, justbewoodsy.com. Table lamp, anthropologie.com. Console table, custom made piece. Pom-pom basket, babasouk.ca.

Pages 200–201: Art on TV, shutter stock/Fresh Stock. Paint, benjamin moore.com (Simply White). Fluted tables, curtains, westelm.com. Lacquer tray, indigo.com. Planter, homesense.ca. Lamp, plant, structube .com. Square basket, zarahome .com. Rug, rugsusa.com. Sofa, eltemkt.com. Throw pillows, shop wildwoven.com. Velvet throw pillow, tonicliving.com. Armchair, article. com. Raffia basket, babasouk.ca. Menorah, cb2.com. Vase, eq3.com. Curtain rod, umbra.com.

Pages 202: (top) Art on TV, shutter stock/Fresh Stock. Lamp, structube .com. Fluted tables, westelm.com. Lacquer tray, indigo.com. Planter, homesense.ca. Square basket, zarahome.com. Rug, rugsusa.com. (bottom) Fluted tables, westelm.com. Lacquer tray, indigo.com. Armchair, article.com.

Pages 203: (top) Art, minted.com. Art light, amazon.com. Fluted tables, westelm.com. Lacquer tray, indigo.com. Armchair, article.com. Menorah, cb2.com. Vase, eq3.com. Planters, homesense.ca. Rug, rugsusa .com. Plant, structube.com. (bottom left) Square basket, zarahome.com.

Pages 204–205: Paint (Simply White and Hilton Head Cream) benjamin moore.com. Stools, bouclair.com. Bar table, wayfair.com. Macrame pendant cord, etsy.com/shop/SitosShop. Sofa, ottoman, article.com. Pendant light, throw pillows, throw blanket, tray, homesense.ca. Oversized art, minted .com. Rug, rugsusa.com. Floor lamp, ikea.com.

Page 206: (bottom left) Sofa, article .com. Rug, rugsusa.com. Floor lamp, ikea.com. Throw blanket, homesense .ca. (top) Curtain, ikea.com. Curtain pull, urbanoutfitters.com. (bottom right) Pendant light, homesense.ca. Bracket, ikea.com.

Page 207: (top) Stools, bouclair.com. Bar table, wayfair.com. Macrame pendant cord, etsy.com/shop/Sitos Shop. Rug, rugsusa.com. Floor lamp, ikea.com. Throw blanket, homesense .ca. (bottom left) Console, homesense .ca. Art, minted.com. (bottom right) Throw pillow, homesense.ca. Curtain, ikea.com. Curtain pull, urbanout fitters.com. Tree plant, wayfair.com.

Page 208: Karlstad sofa, ikea.com. Sofa cover, bemz.com. Green throw pillow, target.com. Waffle throw pillow, homesense.ca.

Page 208: Wall sconces, etsy.com /shop/LightCookie2. Faucet, home depot.com. Mirror, basket, soap holder, soccoliving.ca. Cabinet legs, prettypegs .com. Runner, thrifted. First aid tin, domesticsciencehome.co.uk.

Pages 210–211: Art, society6.com. Raffia baskets, babasouk.ca. Mirror, wayfair.com.

Pages 212: (top) Heart tin, flyingtiger .com. (bottom) Peel-and-stick floor-ing, quadrostyle.com. Toilet paper holder, etsy.com/shop/SlaskaLAB. Basket, homesense.ca

Page 213: Light, mitzi.com. Art, society6 .com. Raffia baskets, babasouk.ca. Mirror, wayfair.com.

Pages 215: Art, society6.com. Toilet paper holder, etsy.com/shop/Slaska LAB. Basket, homesense.ca.

Pages 216–217: (left) Wallpaper, etsy .com/shop/xwallcolors. Shelf, light switch plates, amazon.com. Soap dish, candle, vdevmaison.com. Candleholder, mirror, thrifted. (right) Wallpaper, belartestudio.com. Peel-and-stick tiles, thesmarttiles.com. Mirror, etsy.com/shop/Mirror HomeDecorArt. Hand soap holder, soccoliving.ca.

Page 218: (bottom left) Hand towel holder, anthropologie.com. (top) Light switch plates, amazon.com. (bottom right) Mirror, etsy.com/shop /MirrorHomeDecorArt. Peel-and-stick tiles, thesmarttiles.com. Wallpaper, belartestudio.com.

Page 219: (top left) Wallpaper, etsy .com/shop/xwallcolors. Toilet paper basket, amazon.com. Wall candle-holder, thrifted. (top right) Wallpaper, belartestudio.com. Shelf, homesense .ca. Bud vase, eq3.com. (bottom left) Wallpaper, etsy.com/shop/xwall colors. Shelf, amazon.com. (bottom right) Wallpaper, belartestudio.com. Peel-and-stick tiles, thesmarttiles .com. Mirror, etsy.com/shop/Mirror HomeDecorArt. Hand soap holder, soccoliving.ca.

Page 220: Knobs, homesense.ca. First aid tin, domesticscience.co.uk. Planter, homesense.ca.

Page 221: Wall sconces, etsy.com /shop/LightCookie2, Shower curtain, wayfair.com. Faucet, homedepot.com. Mirror, basket, soap holder, soccoliv ing.ca. Knobs, homesense.ca. Cabinet legs, prettypegs.com. Runner, thrifted.

Page 222: (bottom left) Basket, socco living.ca. Runner, thrifted. Cabinet legs, prettypegs.com. (top) Shower curtain, wayfair.com. Knobs, home sense.ca. Cabinet legs, prettypegs.com. (bottom right) Art, society6.com. First aid tin, domesticscience.co.uk. Planter, homesense.ca.

Page 223: Wall sconces, etsy.com /shop/LightCookie2. Faucet, home depot.com. Mirror, hand soap holder, soccoliving.ca. Tiles, riadtile.com. Toothbrush cup, homesense.ca.

Page 224: Paint (Sulking Pink), farrow-ball.com. Mirror, westmirrors .com. Hemnes shoe cabinet, ikea.com. Raffia basket, babasouk.ca. Bud vases, eq3.com. Pom-pom tassel, etsy.com /shop/XinhandcoGoods.

Page 225: Shelf, ikea.com. Baskets, westelm.com. Planter, eq3.com. Throw pillows, tonicliving.com.

Pages 226–227: Wall hooks, cb2.com. Throw pillows, tonicliving.com. Kallax unit, ikea.com. Baskets, westelm.com. Runner, mellah.ca. Mirror, west mirrors.com. Hemnes shoe cabinet, ikea.com. Raffia basket, babasouk.ca. Bud vases, eq3.com. Pom-pom tassel, etsy.com/shop/XinhandcoGoods. Basket, homesense.ca.

Page 228: (bottom left) Throw pillows, tonicliving.com. (top) Paint (Sulking Pink), farrow-ball.com. Mirror, west mirrors.com. Hemnes shoe cabinet, ikea.com. Raffia basket, babasouk.ca. Bud vases, eq3.com. Pom-pom tassel, etsy.com/shop/XinhandcoGoods. Basket, homesense.ca. Wall light, humanhome.co. (bottom right) Shelf, ikea.com. Baskets, westelm.com.

Page 229: (top) Wall hooks, cb2.com. Throw pillows, tonicliving.com. Kallax unit, ikea.com. Baskets, westelm.com. Runner, mellah.ca. Black rope baskets, hm.com. Rectangle baskets, home sense.ca. White photo box, michaels .com. Bud vases, oakandfort.com. Raffia basket, babasouk.ca. Peach pedestal planter, indigo.com. Gray vase, eq3.com. Blue-gray vase, mud australia.com. (bottom left) Planter, eq3.com. (bottom right) Hemnes shoe cabinet, ikea.com. Pom-pom tassel, etsy.com/shop/XinhandcoGoods.

Pages 230–231: Shelf, etsy.com/shop /KROFTSTUDIO. Hooks, urbanout

Index

ABOUT THE AUTHOR

Alexandra Gater is a stylist and home decor expert, connecting with millions through her home makeover videos on YouTube. She makes design accessible for renters and homeowners alike and believes everyone deserves to live in a beautiful space that feels like home, no matter their budget. Alexandra started her career as the Home Editor for Canada's iconic lifestyle magazine *Chatelaine*, and her work has been featured in *Apartment Therapy*, *Clever by Architectural Digest*, and *Domino Magazine*. She lives in Toronto.